THE WOKE WARPATH

HOW MARXISTS USE RACE AND GENDER TO BREAK AMERICA

Logan Lancing

First edition: May 2022

ISBN: 979-8-9859932-0-2 (Paperback)

ISBN: 979-8-9859932-1-9 (eBook)

Imprint: Independently published

Published by Logan Lancing
Madison, WI

To my son

Seek the truth. Work harder than yesterday. Don't be a communist.

To my wife

This wouldn't have been possible without your love, patience, and support. You mean the world to us.

Contents

"Let your credo be this: Let the lie come into the world, let it even triumph. But not through me."

-Aleksandr Solzhenitsyn (1918-1956),

The Gulag Archipelago

INTRODUCTION

She charged over $300 an hour to tell people they were sexists and racists, and companies like mine clamored for the opportunity to hear her speak. This "Diversity, Equity, and Inclusion" consultant lectured us for hours, making radical claims about power, privilege, and inequality. At the time, I didn't know what I do now. I didn't know that this woman was a communist trying to break America.

This wasn't the first time the telecommunications company I worked for had hired diversity trainers. Before 2019, our human resources department hired consultants who had discussed viewpoint diversity, encouraging employees to celebrate one another for our differences. This training was nothing like that. This woman – we'll call her Claire – wasn't celebrating anything. From capitalism and the police to public schools and equality of opportunity, Claire claimed that the United States was fundamentally broken. She didn't argue that we must be aware of sexism and racism. Instead, she asserted that we all played a part in perpetuating the sexism and racism that she claimed is woven into the very fabric of America. "Sexism and racism are systemic," she explained. "Equity is about disrupting and dismantling systems of oppression to give everyone an equal shot at the same outcome."

We were her new disciples, and Claire spoke to us with the same vigor and moral certainty of a prime-time religious preacher.

We all carried our original sins, and she would baptize us as the latest converts in the church of social justice.

"Our identities lie at the intersection of race, sex, gender, and ability," she said. "As an able-bodied cis white woman, I am both oppressor and oppressed. Today, I speak from my lived experiences as a woman while acknowledging how my intersecting identities perpetuate cisnormativity, whiteness, and injustice."

I surveyed the room, looking for anyone with a dictionary large enough to decipher what I had just heard. Some of my coworkers appeared as confused as I thought they should be, but I was shocked to see a majority with attentive eyes and nodding heads. I had a lot of questions, but I kept quiet, not wanting to humiliate myself in front of my direct reports or senior management.

I left Claire's presentation thinking my company had made an obvious mistake. I thought it inconceivable that our human resources department would knowingly hire such a radical to facilitate discussions about equality, fairness, and difference. Claire had made it clear that the social justice she subscribed to was one of theory and political practice, and she wanted us all to practice her politics too. My company requested feedback, so I indicated that we should avoid hiring Claire's firm again. In my mind, colleagues would inundate our human resources department with similar responses. That, I thought, would bring an end to the sermonizing.

A few months later, I received an email inviting me to participate in our company's very first "antiracist book club." The CEO's message struck me as odd. Firstly, we had never done a book club before, and our CEO wasn't one to pay people to read. Secondly, as a middle manager, I thought I had a good sense of our company culture. Not once had I heard of accusations of sexism or racism from my staff or any other. I knew my colleagues were against racism, so I didn't understand why we all needed to read a book to explore a problem we didn't have. I thought I might be missing something, so again I dropped my questions and concerns for fear of humiliation or worse.

In my book club invitation, Mark, my CEO, had stated explicitly that our company would adopt a culture of antiracism. He expected us all to become antiracists. At this point, I started to think that "antiracist" may not mean what I thought it did. I read Ibram X. Kendi's *How to Be an Antiracist* the week before our first book club meeting and found my suspicion was well placed. Kendi's antiracist framework flew in the face of the liberalism I have valued all my life. Kendi opposes equality of opportunity, neutral principles of constitutional law, and color-blindness. He openly advocates for discrimination, using "equity" as a redistribution vehicle to force equal outcomes between groups. "The defining question," he writes, "is whether the discrimination is creating equity or inequity. If discrimination is creating equity, then it is antiracist. If discrimination is creating inequity, then it is racist."[1]

My team was diverse, but it didn't reflect the demographic representation of America's various racial categories. I employed more women than men and more white Americans than black. If I were to practice Kendi's antiracism, I would need to discriminate against qualified female and white applicants until all groups on my team matched the demographic representation of the greater population. That, in my view, was racist and sexist. Mark couldn't possibly be advocating for something so illegal.

I thought I must be misunderstanding Kendi's work, so I reread it, taking meticulous notes and engaging with the text at a level I thought I had left behind in college. Again, I reached the same conclusion. He was a radical who attributed all group differences to racism or sexism. His antiracist framework abandoned liberalism, objectivity, and reason in favor of authoritarianism, subjectivity, and insanity. For all his flaws, I knew Mark was not a dull man. I could not understand why he was pushing such nonsense onto a healthy workforce. Where was all of this coming from?

I found my answer during our first book club meeting. An employee – we'll call her Mary – had volunteered to facilitate the discussion. She kicked off the session by thanking our CEO for being an "ally" for racial justice. "We met with Mark late last year to discuss police brutality and racial injustice," she said. "As a white woman, I could no longer remain silent while the black and brown community shoulder the weight of injustice in our city and workforce. Mark has made an organizational commitment to diversity, equity, inclusion, and antiracism, and today we all begin to do the hard work of combatting discrimination and white supremacy culture. Thank you, Mark, for being an ally and committed antiracist leader."

I now knew what had happened. A small group of employees had approached Mark and convinced him that he needed to radically reorganize his company's mission and values to combat "systemic" and "institutionalized" racism. I now understood that Claire's presentation months earlier hadn't been a mistake – it had been an intentional step to introduce a new organizing principle into the company. An illiberal regime was taking root before my eyes, cloaked in the moralistic language of social justice activism.

I placed my notes back into my binder. Mary and others spoke with an authority they did not have, but I knew this wasn't the place for discussion or debate. I knew Kendi used circular reasoning and false choices throughout his book, and Mary would likely do the same. She had captured Mark, and challenging Mary and her circle of antiracist radicals was to challenge already foregone conclusions.

A few employees were far braver than I, perhaps because their inexperience blinded them to the game we were now playing or because they had but a single mouth to feed. Phil, a new hire working debt collection, got straight to the point – "This guy [Kendi] says discrimination is OK if you do it to the right people, but I think that's wrong. We should treat everyone equally."

Without a moment's hesitation, Mary responded. "I think the critical thing to remember is that marginalized communities have never been treated equally in this country. As antiracists, we aren't called to discriminate against people. We are called to disrupt and dismantle the systems that create inequities in our workplaces, schools, and government."

Mary's reply was what I expected to hear after spending so much time engaging with Kendi's work. For her, everything was black and white; power and oppression. Like Kendi, she thought all disparities in outcome were the result of systems of power privileging some while marginalizing others. She supported discrimination because her worldview demanded it. Phil was outgunned, lost in the weeds of a language he did not understand. A fatal trap had been set – who could be against antiracism?

What started as diversity training and an innocent-sounding book club invitation quickly evolved into a new illiberal orthodoxy, headed by a Diversity, Equity, and Inclusion regime that poisoned everything. Our culture had previously been one of optimism, hard work, friendship, and fun. Now, suspicion, anxiety, and endless conversations about race, sex, gender, and politics dominated our days. Employees tiptoed around language as if they were avoiding landmines. Our newly minted DEI committee directed employees to place gender pronouns in our email signatures and zoom profiles. The untouchable priestly class then directed us to open meetings with "trigger warnings" and "safe space" commitments. Whereas our workplace had once been apolitical, we now received emails about supporting specific causes and voting for party-approved political candidates. Some of our meetings were now racially segregated – deliberately.

What happened at my workplace is happening in workplaces across the country. It's also happening in schools, government, and healthcare. Small groups of radical activists are forcing people to practice a form of social justice that most people find unrecognizable. These moral busybodies marry their ideology with political activism, breaking institutions in the name of "social justice." People are afraid to speak out against this new orthodoxy for fear of losing their jobs or being ostracized as sexists or racists. Many people know something is terribly wrong, but they can't put their finger on it. They don't understand why this is happening – why activists are so relentless in their attempt to convince everyone America is irredeemable, when, to the contrary, the country is objectively less racist and sexist than it has ever been. The fantasy world described by Claire, Kendi, and Mary doesn't match reality.

I put the pieces together after the first book club meeting. Claire, Kendi, and Mary were not outliers. They represented an accurate depiction of what social justice looks like in the 21st century. Their theories of race, sex, and gender were not radical in the sense that they departed from what other leading social justice advocates were preaching and practicing. Their theories represented the norm, which was antithetical to liberalism and capitalism – the two most significant organizing frameworks ever devised by man.

I am a husband, a father, and a patriot. I love America and sincerely appreciate her history, people, and what she represents. Over a year ago, I set out to write this book because I was as confused as one possibly could be. I didn't know half of the words Claire used in her presentation. I didn't understand how Kendi could get so much wrong and sit at the top of the New York Times Best Sellers list. I was beside myself when my company said I should try to avoid "hiring another white guy." After I noticed the same racially charged language, concepts, and practices enter my children's school district, I decided enough was enough. I've spent the last year decoding the texts, language, and rituals of those that practice this new form of "Critical Social Justice". I've discovered why race and gender are breaking America.

In this book, I explain where Critical Social Justice comes from and define the Critical Thinkers that practice it. Claire, Kendi, and Mary view the world through a very different lens than your typical person. They didn't arrive at their radical interpretations of society in a vacuum. The words they use have long histories and specific meanings, and they use them to coerce, punish, and program people to think and act in revolutionary ways. These radicals practice an illiberal political tradition founded in Marxism more than a century ago. This tradition now dominates our institutions, threatening to destroy the most unique experiment ever attempted by mankind.

After defining what a Critical Thinker is and why they view the world in the way they do, I explain how these men and women have forced themselves into positions of power. I detail how Critical Thinkers make their way into your workplaces, school boards, and city councils by morally compromising those in their crosshairs, using Diversity, Equity, and Inclusion to "disrupt and dismantle" everything.

Most importantly, I tackle the radical claims of Critical Thinkers and detail how they use these claims to break society. It is not a coincidence that, as commitments to social justice intensify, our cities become less safe, our schools become political factories, and the fabric holding everything together is being torn apart. After reading this book, you will understand how and why race and gender are breaking America, why statues of Washington, Lincoln, and Jefferson must fall, why language must be redefined, why we must all be antiracists, and why reality no longer matters. You will understand why politicians are defunding the police and legalizing crime in cities like San Francisco, why teachers are programming children to become political activists in New York, and why the most progressive among us are rushing to dismantle women's rights.

Two years ago, I had no idea what I was looking at. I do now. We are witnessing an attempt to usher in a Marxian revolutionary struggle to overthrow America. We are witnessing a hostile communist takeover.

CHAPTER ONE

CRITICAL THINKERS

This isn't your grandmother's social justice movement. In California, 3rd graders are deconstructing their racial identities in math class. They complete "identity maps" to learn which children have "power and privilege" and which do not.[2]

In New York City, a high school principal asks parents to become "white traitors." A white traitor is someone who "actively refuses complicity" and whose intention is to "subvert authority" and "dismantle institutions."[3]

In Seattle, government agencies hold racially segregated meetings. These "listening sessions" are a tool for dismantling "institutional privileges and systemic inequities embedded in the current socio-political conditions that influence and affect our institutions."[4]

It's hard to imagine how children might benefit from learning to place social significance onto their skin color. Most people think it wrong to ask kids to associate the color of their skin with anything more than what it is – melanin. It's even harder to imagine what good can come from telling one child that her classmates hold power and privilege over her – and that these classmates are her oppressors.

For a particular type of person, asking children to identify their power and privilege is a necessary method to eliminate the inequality they see in the world. Asking parents to "dismantle institutions" is the only way to break a corrupt system and rebuild society. Telling people that they can only attend a certain meeting with others that share the same skin color is a progressive form of social justice.

The people who think in this way and do these things are generally considered "woke." Someone who is woke is said to have awoken to the injustice of society. A woke person looks behind the curtains to find the racism and prejudice in the world that is invisible to everyone else.

Whereas a business might appear to give every applicant a fair shot at the job, that business has hired nine white people to fill the last ten open positions. On paper, the business is doing everything legally. The human resources department has audited the company's hiring practices and found no evidence of discrimination. The awakened mind doesn't buy it; it is skeptical. The woke assume discrimination is at play. The company is producing an inequality of outcome between groups. Something fishy is going on, and the woke make it their mission to root it out.

But the word "woke" isn't a specific enough term to describe the worldview of the people advocating for a color-conscious, hyper racialized society. The people who think we should prioritize skin color, dismantle our institutions, and get back to racial segregation are not just "woke" thinkers. They are "Critical Thinkers."

"Critical Thinkers" practice "Critical Thinking" – but not the kind of critical thinking with which we are all accustomed. As traditionally understood, critical thinking is a fundamental tool required for any citizen to participate in a well-developed society. Learning how to think critically is to recognize faulty arguments and lousy evidence when making decisions or advocating for change. To think critically, one analyzes the facts, throws away one's assumptions, and develops arguments substantiated by logic and sound evidence. Every human is capable of coming to their conclusions by way of critical thinking. One simply needs to ask questions and think about how one knows what one knows.

By contrast, a Critical Thinker practices Critical Thinking. Rather than trying to understand how we know what we know, a Critical Thinker tries to understand how systems of power influence and determine the course and development of society. Critical Thinking is the practice of analyzing and deconstructing systems of power – not knowledge.

Critical Thinkers believe power to be the fundamental organizing principle of society. That is to say; Critical Thinkers believe a hierarchy of power permeates all of society and determines who gets access to societal benefits and privileges and who does not. This power differentiates between the "oppressor" and the "oppressed." The more power one has, the more access society grants them. The less power someone has, the more disadvantaged and oppressed they are. Critical Thinkers argue that society locks us into a zero-sum game wherein all players struggle to secure a finite amount of power.

The Critical Thinker's job is to critique this systemic power against a vision of a power-neutral system. This critique allows the Critical Thinker to find imbalances of power and prescribe activism to tear down the structures and inputs that are creating the imbalance in the first place. Critical Thinkers call the process of interrupting and breaking power structures "disrupting and dismantling." Critical Thinkers argue that, by disrupting the power structure's inputs and dismantling the mechanism through which power operates, one can free people from oppression. In the end, everyone can be made equal in a power-neutral society.

Critical Thinkers have a lot to say about America's institutions. They believe the United States to be one of the most corrupt, racist, sexist, and bigoted countries ever to have existed. Their critique is damning. Critical Thinkers argue that a power-hierarchy is woven into the very fabric of America. This hierarchy determines the outcomes of each of our lives, using the inputs of race, gender, ethnicity, and sexuality to sort us out. Those deemed worthy of total freedom are privileged by this system. Those deemed unworthy do not have an equal shot at making their dreams a reality.

Today, Critical Thinkers are the masterminds of the various sociopolitical movements tearing the United States apart. They are on the warpath, undermining our systems of law and policing, brainwashing children, and creating an authoritarian state in which viewpoint diversity and the truth will no longer be tolerated. And they are doing this all on purpose.

Critical Thinking is Marxist Thinking

Critical Thinking effectively began with German philosopher Karl Marx in the 19th century. Marx believed that history progressed in stages. A revolutionary exchange of power brought about by class conflicts and changing modes of production marked these progressions. Marx argued that the capitalist ruling class of his day (the bourgeoisie) had brought about the current stage of history – capitalism – by revolutionizing the organization of human labor during the industrial revolution. These capitalists had used their factories, machines, and capital to extract surplus value from the working class (the proletariat). With this surplus value, capitalists hoarded power, restructuring society to benefit the few at the expense of the many.

Marx predicted that the next stage of history would end this unequal system. He argued that the inequality of the capitalist system would generate too many contradictions to be ignored. While capitalists hoarded an ever-mounting share of wealth, a growing number of people would be forced into the working class and become poor. While the select few would live lives of leisure and luxury, the many would work longer hours in ever more filthy and dangerous conditions. The voice of the minority would increasingly dominate the powerless and oppressed majority.

For Marx, capitalism would fall when the working class developed "class consciousness." Workers would become conscious of these increasingly apparent contradictions and decide that their objective material conditions were too brutal to bear. Those with a common grievance and class consciousness would eventually engage in a collective struggle to overthrow capitalism through violent revolution. In so doing, these revolutionaries would bring about the socialist stage of history in which a centralized state redistributed everything in the economy, ensuring fairness among all peoples by guaranteeing equality of outcomes. Eventually, as the system perfected itself, the state would no longer be necessary. The last stage of history – communism – would begin.

Only by grouping individuals into a common class struggle by accelerating their shared grievances could the communist revolution take place. A sufficient number of people would need to wake up to their current condition. Workers would need to realize all of the ways capitalism fell short of the promises of communism and then take action to make communism a reality. All of this, according to Marx, was inevitable.

But Marx was wrong. Workers weren't developing Marx's predicted class consciousness in the 19th century. Instead, workers within liberal capitalist systems were enjoying previously unseen standards of living. These liberal capitalist systems figured out ways to mitigate the negative aspects of capitalism and protect workers from Marx's predicted spiraling conditions. By protecting individual rights and adding profit incentives, free peoples were motivated to generate more material wealth than the world had ever seen. This tide lifted all boats, and even the poor working class within the framework of liberal capitalism could be considered filthy rich compared to those operating outside of it. The supply of grievance was insufficient to fuel the flames of revolution.

Critical Theory: The Long March Through the Institutions

Karl Marx died in a world absent of his global working-class revolution. But he didn't die in a world absent his predictions.

Many early 20th century philosophers bought into the philosophical tradition that had become Marxism. These Marxist philosophers worked to understand why Marx's global revolution had never materialized in Western societies. At the time, there was a suspicion that Karl Marx must have missed something. There must have been a mechanism preventing the global worker's revolution from occurring, something hindering the development of a global class consciousness.

The founder of the Italian Communist Party, Antonio Gramsci, argued that this previously unaccounted for mechanism was something called "cultural hegemony." Gramsci thought that the ruling middle class was using Western culture to steer the working class away from its best interests; the ruling class thus masked the contradictions that would catalyze a revolution. Gramsci theorized that the middle class controlled social institutions that fed the working class the ideas, beliefs, norms, and values that the middle class wanted lower-class workers to have. Workers' minds were being hijacked and made to believe that capitalism was good for them.

Gramsci believed the working class had internalized Western culture and become blind to their subordination. This oppressed group had developed a "false consciousness"; they accepted the dominant narratives of the liberal middle class as the only genuine way of understanding and interacting with the world. They couldn't see the possibility of something better because cultural institutions – the family, education, religion, politics, the media, and popular culture – subdued the revolutionary spirit. This cultural hegemony (dominance) fed subordinate groups a way of life to keep those groups in their oppressed state by smoke and mirrors rather than force. This new approach to understanding class conflict was called neo-Marxism. Gramsci critiqued Marxist theory and then applied it to culture. The aim was now to develop a cultural consciousness that would lead to an economic one.

Gramsci argued for a counter-culture that could undermine and replace the centers of cultural production in Western liberal democracies with neo-Marxism. In 1915 he wrote, "Socialism is precisely the religion that must overwhelm Christianity... In the new order, Socialism will triumph by first capturing the culture via the infiltration of schools, universities, churches, and the media by transforming the consciousness of society."[5] In other words, Gramsci was advocating for neo-Marxist intellectuals to infiltrate institutions, transform their culture, and produce a new cultural hegemony in Western society. Gramsci wanted neo-Marxists to morally bankrupt Western liberal democracy and to disrupt and dismantle it from within.

Other neo-Marxist thinkers in the early 20th century had reached similar conclusions. In the 1920s and 30s, these thinkers coalesced and founded the Institute for Social Research in Frankfurt, Germany (The Frankfurt School). There, they critiqued Marxist theory further and developed Critical Theory, a tool used to dismantle the cultural hegemony of the Western liberal middle class.

Traditional theories seek to describe something and understand how and why it works in the way it does. For instance, Albert Einstein gave the world a special and general theory of relativity. We use these theories today to predict the existence of black holes and understand the behavior of planets in orbit. We use them to adjust for the time dilation experienced by the high and fast-moving satellites that constitute our Global Positioning System (GPS). Clocks tick faster in Earth orbit relative to us on the surface. Without the understanding granted to us by Einstein's theories, your GPS would be off within 2 minutes. The global positioning system would be worthless within a few days.[6]

But Einstein's theories tell us nothing about what gravity, energy, mass, and speed should be; they only describe Einstein's understanding of what those things are. A critical theory is less concerned with how and why things are the way they are, and more concerned with how they should be. A critical theory critiques phenomena against a moral (or "normative") vision of society and describes how the current phenomena under study falls short of this moral vision. A critical theory prescribes activism to disrupt and dismantle the phenomena in question to reconstruct it in alignment with this moral ideal.[7]

Critical Theorists (those who practice Critical Theory) believe that one must ruthlessly criticize society to discover how systems of power, exploitation, and oppression affect those within that society. The point is less to understand why things are the way they are, and more to "problematize" those things you wish to be different. To problematize something is to make visible all of the ways in which that thing is maintaining the status quo; to uncover how the thing you are critiquing is causing oppression; to point out how that thing falls short of one's moral vision. Once one has problematized a specific phenomenon, one must seek to disrupt and dismantle it to stop the reproduction of oppression and correct for the power imbalances one has determined are there.

Armed with Critical Theory, neo-Marxist Critical Theorists set out to criticize liberal democratic societies for all of the ways those societies did not live up to the moral promise of communism. These first-generation Critical Theorists spread their practice to the United States after Hitler's rise to power in the 1930s. They would spend time conducting their research and developing their Critical Theory in New York, Los Angeles, and Washington DC. In these places, Critical Theory would capture the imagination of professors, college students, and radicals alike.

A New Revolutionary Avant-Garde

By the mid-20th century, it was clear that the Western working class was not going to develop a collective class consciousness on its own. Instead, it seemed that Western citizens had developed a false consciousness. Westerners believed the system was working in their interest. They had access to jobs, were able to put food on the table, and raise families in relative peace. The neo-Marxist Critical Theorists understood this fact. As the father of Critical Theory, Max Horkheimer, stated in an interview in 1969, "[Karl Marx] believed that this capitalist society would necessarily have to be overcome by the solidarity spelled by the increasing immiseration of the working class. This idea is wrong. This society in which we live does not immiserate the workers but helps them to build a better life."[8]

Capitalism had survived two World Wars and the Great Depression. If the workers of the world hadn't united when the system was stretched to the breaking point, when would they? Critical Theorists of the second half of the 20th century believed they could dig deeper. There must be an angle they hadn't yet considered, a key to unlocking the revolutionary struggle.

Herbert Marcuse was a German Critical Theorist who taught political theory at Columbia, Harvard, Brandeis, and the University of California San Diego. Marcuse built on the work of his predecessors by further defining how neo-Marxists might unseat the cultural hegemony of liberal capitalist systems. Like Gramsci, Marcuse believed that the key to unlocking the revolution lay in the minds of the oppressed. He argued that teaching people to develop a radical consciousness with Critical Theory (critical consciousness) would lead to the dissolution of society's "moral fiber." That is to say, people who perceived the world the way Marcuse did would become so horrified by their subjugation they would no longer be able to function within it. This development would catalyze a "biological need for freedom"[9] from repressive society.

"A society depends on the relatively stable and calculable sanity of the people, sanity defined as the regular, socially coordinated functioning of mind and body – especially at work, in the shops and offices, but also at leisure and fun. Moreover, a society also demands to a considerable extent, belief in one's beliefs (which is part of the required sanity)."[10]

Marcuse argued that advanced capitalist systems could be made unstable by taking advantage of the dysfunction caused by such realizations. The "dissolution of social morality," Marcuse writes, "may manifest in a collapse of work discipline, slowdown, spread of disobedience to rules and regulations, wildcat strikes, boycotts, sabotage, [and] gratuitous acts of noncompliance."[11] The dissolution of the sanity of everyday people would lead to "discontent and mental sickness," and "inefficiency, resistance to work, refusal to perform, negligence, [and] indifference."[12] A system with this level of dysfunction, Marcuse argued, would be ripe for a revolutionary takeover.

But the neo-Marxist Critical Theorists needed first to abandon the idea that the working class could become the first movers in a modern communist revolution. These workers were not being made miserable. They were prosperous. If the goal was to capitalize on the dissolution of the "relatively stable and calculable sanity of the people," Critical Theorists needed to leave behind what was now considered a stabilizing and conservative anti-revolutionary force.

Marcuse explicitly targeted college students and "ghetto" populations to become his new revolutionary class.

"Very different from the revolution at previous stages of history, this opposition is directed against the totality of a well-functioning, prosperous society – a protest against its Form – the commodity form of men and things, against the imposition of false values and a false morality. This new consciousness and the instinctual rebellion isolate such opposition from the masses and from the majority of organized labor, the integrated majority, and make for the concentration of radical politics in active minorities, mainly among the young middle-class intelligentsia, and among the ghetto populations."[13]

Young college students (the militant intelligentsia) and "ghetto" populations needed to be pulled out of the stable working class and radicalized with neo-Marxist Critical Theory. College students were prime targets because of their age and location. These students had open views of the world, considered life a ball of endless possibility, and, for the first time, were isolated from the values of their parents. They were inexperienced and knew less about how the real world worked and more about what they thought it should look like. In short, neo-Marxists like Marcuse could program these students easily before sending them back into society to work as economists, business owners, government officials, and CEOs. Once programmed, the militant intelligentsia would radicalize the "ghetto" populations situated mainly in big cities. Together, these energetic groups could be "easily organized and directed" into a struggle against "targets of vital economic and political importance."[14]

To radicalize these young college students and ghetto populations, Critical Theorists needed to train them to develop a critical consciousness; a realization that society oppressed people along not just the line of class but also along the lines of race, sex, and ethnicity. Critical Theorists like Marcuse needed these populations to adopt Critical Theory and believe that Western society was rotten to the core with racism, sexism, and oppression. Marcuse needed students and minorities to wake up – to become woke – and realize how oppressed they were before heading back into the working class to disrupt and dismantle it.

Situation Critical: Critical Theory and Postmodernism

Neo-Marxist like Antonio Gramsci and Herbert Marcuse argued that Western liberal democracy kept the minds of potential revolutionaries trapped in a system of spoon-fed values and beliefs. Countries like the United States of America were prosperous, and Americans were happy to go to work, come home, kick off their shoes, play with the kids, and watch football. Marcuse contended that Americans just didn't understand how unhappy and oppressed they really were.

Critical Theorists needed to raise a critical consciousness in young intellectuals and minorities to destabilize the Western liberal-democratic and capitalist system. They needed to generate fissures in the system with a steady supply of grievance and discontent. To sow the seeds of revolution, Critical Theorists wanted to inspire those in their crosshairs to conclude that the beliefs and values they held were false, and that the assumptions and orthodoxy of Critical Theory were correct. The Critical Theorists needed postmodernism.

Postmodernism is a philosophical movement that dominated the academy in the late 20th century. It is characterized by its ruthless criticism of the modern world. To be specific, postmodernism questions how we know what we know and concludes that there is no such thing as "the truth" that humans can access.

People built the modern world on the idea that there are universal truths out in the world, and every human can find them. Through reason, rationality, empiricism, and the scientific method, human beings can understand the world as it is. Enlightenment thinkers like John Locke, Francis Bacon, Adam Smith, and Rene Descartes laid the groundwork for a liberal-democratic, economic, and scientific tradition that pulled an untold number of peoples out of abject suffering and poverty. Western countries used Enlightenment tools to reason their way to individual rights, democracy, freedom of speech and religion, and free-market economies. People were free to reason their way to conclusions with a universally accessible toolkit rather than being led to "the truth" by superstition or those with privileged knowledge. With this freedom, Western countries built the modern world.

Whereas the Enlightenment toolkit helped build the modern world, the postmodern toolkit would tear it down. Postmodern thinkers argued that reason, objectivity, and the scientific method were tools to be discarded. There was no such thing as an objective "truth" that one could find in the world; there were only subjective "truths."

Postmodernists sought to "deconstruct" truth claims. In their view, "the truth" was arrived at when someone with power decided to use that power to make something true. Those in privileged and powerful positions – scientists, doctors, lawyers, politicians – guided various discourses (the way we talk about things) to "the truth" as they wanted it to be.

Postmodern thinker Michael Foucault called this phenomenon "power-knowledge." He argued that knowledge validated power, which was then used to generate more knowledge to validate itself. That is to say, various scientific, economic, and political disciplines used knowledge to assume power, and those disciplines used their increased power to generate more knowledge that further strengthened and centralized their control.

For Foucault, knowledge and power dictate how we interact with our institutions, develop theories, and talk about things. Knowledge and power intertwine in a positive feedback loop that allows dominant epistemologies (which describe how we know what we know) to emerge. Knowledge was not objective but subjective; a result of dominant and privileged groups asserting their power to tell everyone else: what is right and what is wrong; how one is to behave and how one is not to behave; and how one is to view the world and how one is not to view the world.

With this power, dominant groups baked their subjective knowledge into society to ensure control over all other forms of knowledge. For Foucault, there was no such thing as an objective fact; there was only subjective knowledge that produced personal facts.

Postmodern thinkers argued that because knowledge is subjective and no one knows "the truth," everything in society is a social construction. Race, class, sex, and gender are not "real things." These categories are socially constructed by those in power to control how people act and think in the world. One's identity results from societal norms, assumptions, and pressures imposed on a person trapped in a zero-sum conflict with others. Postmodernism is the nihilistic belief that nothing matters; that instead it's all about power, privilege, oppression, and control.

Postmodernism was a tool for deconstructing everything about the world and tearing it down, offering nothing in return. Postmodernism said nothing about what the world ought to be. Furthermore, because there was no such thing as "the truth," postmodernism was relegated to academic circles where it deconstructed itself. It was useless. That is, it was useless until Critical Theorists applied postmodernism[15] to their Critical methods and used it to critique society against "the truth" of their moral vision.

The Rise of the Critical Thinker

Critical Theorists spent the 20th century arguing about how to bring about the communist revolution. They settled on a plan to seize the means of Western cultural production to hollow institutions out from within. Critical Theorists needed to subdivide the working class by helping college students and minorities develop a critical consciousness. They sought to sow discontent and outrage in those groups to destabilize the backbone of society and make the whole system susceptible to collapse. And they did just that.

Armed with postmodern tools, the Critical Theorists of the late 20th century saturated academia with new Critical Theories that deconstructed race, sex, and power with the explicit aim of developing a critical consciousness in college students, minorities and, eventually, everyone else. Chief among these new critical theories were Critical Race Theory (CRT) and Queer Theory.

CRT stipulated that America was "institutionally" and "systemically" racist. Rather than critiquing all of the ways culture blinded the working class to their subjugation, CRT critiqued all of the ways society blinded everyone to the oppression of non-white peoples. The activists that developed and practiced CRT argued that equality of opportunity, neutral principles of constitutional law, and rights – especially private property – were nothing more than white supremacist tools used to subjugate black Americans and keep them permanently situated in a lower class. For Critical Race Theorists, race is *the lens* through which we must view the world.

Queer Theory maintained that sex and gender are nothing more than social constructs used to maintain "heteronormativity" and "cisnormativity." That is to say, Queer Theorists critiqued all of the ways society marginalized anyone who was not heterosexual or anyone whose "gender identity" didn't match their "sex assigned at birth." The activists "queering" things challenged the idea that sex and gender mean anything at all. They argued that one's gender identity and sex are malleable; men can become women, and women can become men. For Queer Theorists, gender is *the lens* through which we must view the world.

Critical Criminologists argued that crime should be legal because breaking societal laws was done in an act of open resistance against an oppressive capitalist system. Those practicing Critical Pedagogy argued that children's classrooms must be made political to overthrow the dominant, oppressive narratives of a liberal democratic order. Chronically obese women now grace the covers of magazines as shining examples of "health at any size" because of Critical Fat Studies.

These postmodern neo-Marxist critical theories of identity sow division and victimhood into society by placing people into a life-or-death struggle for power. Various identity groups compete to position themselves on the top of the pyramid of oppression – a place of "lived experience" and moral authority that grants the victor control over what "truth" is to be accepted and what facts are to be discarded. Individualism is made subordinate to group membership, and all groups are expected to disrupt and dismantle everything that threatens their worldview. If one's life is challenging or unfair, it's because some nefarious system has made it so. Everyone has a "positionality" within a "matrix of oppression" from which they must fight for "liberation."

For decades, college students have learned these various theories in gender studies, African American studies, women's studies, history, psychology, sociology, political science, and teacher certification programs. These graduates – the militant intelligentsia – have gone into the world and spread postmodern neo-Marxist Critical Theory into every mainstream American institution, aiming to create a new cultural hegemony to displace liberalism. They are Critical Thinkers seeking to develop a critical consciousness in everyone by spreading the virus that is Critical Thinking.

A Critical Thinker is a postmodern neo-Marxist practitioner of critical theories. A Critical Thinker critiques all of society against their "normative" vision of what society should look like (socialism and then communism) and actively seeks to disrupt and dismantle everything. Critical Thinkers are radical activists driving the racial, gender, and class divisions that dominate our news headlines and political debates. Today's social justice movement is little more than a Marxist revolutionary struggle.

Karl Marx said that "the philosophers have only interpreted the world, in various ways. The point, however, is to change it." Critical Thinkers are doing just that. They are activists who use their various critical and postmodern theories to make radical claims about society. With these claims, they bully their way into positions of power through coercive and authoritarian means. Once Critical Thinkers disrupt an institution and secure governing authority, they dismantle it in accordance with their ideology. The point is: to disrupt and dismantle everything; to practice Critical Social Justice; and to break society and force the newest iterations of communism on us all.

This strategy has been incredibly successful. Critical Thinkers are responsible for defunding the police and legalizing crime. They are responsible for teaching kids that life is all about power and privilege. They are increasingly responsible for determining what is true and suppressing the voice of anyone who would challenge their control.

Critical Thinkers are on the Woke Warpath to dismantle the pillars that uphold Western civilization. Because of them, people are increasingly unable to share a single political view that won't be deemed "racist," "sexist," or "bigoted" if it isn't in agreement with a Critical Thinker's revolutionary worldview. Our social media companies label everything that doesn't align with Critical Thinking as "hate speech." We no longer have freedom of religion; we must accept the Critical Thinker's orthodoxy at our workplace, in our schools, and our community. The rule of law increasingly means "I can do that, but you can't." Equality no longer matters – everyone must be forced to be equal (equity). The church of Critical Thinking has wedded the State – including the law, the military, and even the White House. Critical Thinkers will not tolerate anyone who isn't thinking "critically" about the world.

The behavior of Critical Thinkers is predictable. They introduce a radical claim into the world, steal moral authority, use coercion and speech suppression to force everyone to accept their claims as true, and use their viral position to begin breaking things they don't like. They are authoritarians obsessed with capturing power and forcing everyone to play their illiberal game.

Throughout this book, I tackle the radical claims of Critical Thinkers, demonstrating that their claims cannot be believed by a thinking person. Critical Thinkers argue from conclusions rather than to them. They begin with a set of presuppositions – that America is sexist and racist – and then argue backward, cherry-picking univariate models to make their analysis. They live and play in a fantasy world where lies go unpunished, and no one can challenge their ruleset.

I also detail what the dismantling process looks like and share just how much damage has already been done. It cannot be overstated that Critical Thinkers serve only two purposes; help others develop a critical consciousness and break everything. Unfortunately, they are exceptionally good at doing both of these things when unchallenged.

America is not beyond saving, and it is in everyone's best interests to recognize what is happening for what it really is. This isn't "identity politics" or "those silly woke kids on campus." This is a radical attempt to break capitalism and liberal democracy.

Chapter 2 of this book explores what disrupting and dismantling an institution looks like in detail. In 2017, Evergreen State College erupted into chaos when a white teacher refused to remain absent on campus during a day where no white people were allowed to be there. Students rioted, locked campus administrators in a room, and assumed complete control of the campus.

Chapter 3 examines how Critical Thinkers use radical claims about race and gender to disrupt and dismantle institutions more broadly. We explore how a few radicals can poison an organization with these claims, usurp power, silence or eliminate dissidents, and dismantle everything.

In Chapters 4, 6, and 8, we examine the three most disruptive radical claims that Critical Thinkers have used to secure authority and determine how we police our streets, educate our children, and decide what the truth is. I demonstrate why these radical claims are absurd and offer an alternative explanation for why "their truth" is not "the truth."

In Chapters 5, 7, and 9, we explore what Critical Thinkers are doing to dismantle our police departments, schools, and women's rights. I introduce the literature Critical Thinkers draw from to explain why they believe what they believe, and do the things they do.

In Chapter 10, I explain just how deep this rabbit hole is. I argue that, as a society, we have two choices we have in front of us; either we let Critical Thinkers continue on their Woke Warpath, or we push back and fight against the dismantling of the liberal-democratic order. I argue that what we have is not only worth saving – it is the only path a true social justice warrior could ever consider. The Woke Warpath must be stopped.

CHAPTER TWO

EVERGREEN STATE COLLEGE: DISMANTLED

> "Here is a riddle not for us contemporaries to figure out: Why is Germany allowed to punish its evildoers and Russia is not? What kind of disastrous path lies ahead of us if we do not have the chance to purge ourselves of that putrefaction rotting inside our body? What, then, can Russia teach the world?"
>
> –Aleksandr Solzhenitsyn,
> *The Gulag Archipelago*

In 1964, the Council of Presidents of Washington State's university system issued a report that noted a geographic imbalance in the distribution of state universities and colleges.[16] Western Washington, the most populous part of the State and the fastest-growing, could not meet the upcoming years' anticipated enrollments.

By 1975, the current system would have 17,000 additional students that it could not accommodate. Boeing had recently won a design competition for a supersonic airliner, the Boeing 2707, and intended on manufacturing the vehicle near Seattle. When the Vietnam War ended, "thousands of additional young men" would "march back to college classrooms under provisions of the GI Bill of Rights."[17] Enrollments for Washington's state universities would grow by over 30 percent, followed by community college growth of 122 percent. For these reasons, Washington's legislature would develop plans for a new college. Dr. Garret Heyns, the President of the Southwestern Washington State College Committee, stated in 1967 that, "Not since the early days of statehood has the Legislature of the State of Washington been called upon to make such an important decision on higher education as that which is being considered here tonight."[18]

Evergreen State College, calling Olympia, Washington its home, opened its doors to students in 1971. Not only would the new liberal arts institution help address the influx of future Boeing employees (although the Boeing 2707 project was scrapped), veterans, and intellectually curious students of all kinds, but it would also become the proving ground for a remarkable experiment in higher education. From its inception, Evergreen State College wasn't going to be like other colleges. It was to be a "flexible and sophisticated educational instrument," one that would "unshackle our educational thinking from traditional patterns."[19] For those who had a hand in creating the college, Evergreen State College was to be an extraordinary place where learning, governance, and power relations were all done differently. It was to be a place where the rigid institutional norms of other colleges were replaced with a new framework that allowed students to engage with their learning in a unique, experiential, and interdisciplinary way.

At Evergreen, students do not receive grades. There are no departments. Students don't enroll in courses like they typically would at other liberal arts colleges. Whereas an incoming freshman at a traditional institution might enroll in disconnected introductory coursework in economics, history, and physics, each class covering only the fundamental principles specific to that discipline, Evergreen students enroll in all-encompassing programs that incorporate multiple disciplines. These students learn about and approach topics and issues from multiple perspectives. Instead of filling one's class schedule for an upcoming semester with a patchwork of 3 and 4 credit classes, students at Evergreen choose one program each semester through which they, their 25 or so classmates, and multiple instructors endeavor to learn about topics and issues through a broad multi-disciplinary framework. For example, a student enrolled in the 16-credit course *America in Translation: History, Culture, Theory* would learn about American culture by exploring U.S. history, cultural studies, comparative literature, and media studies.[20] Two instructors teach the course: a professor specializing in U.S. History, African American history, and American studies, and another specializing in writing, comparative literature, film, and visual culture. A typical week for an Evergreen student enrolled in a program like this might include multiple lectures, workshops, seminars, laboratory, tutoring, and study time. Small cohorts of students and professors navigate the program together, developing bonds that are hard to achieve in traditional colleges where each class may have dozens or even hundreds of students. Overall, with programs and coursework structured in this way, students receive a one-of-a-kind education as they approach their curriculum by immersing themselves in a learning experience that better reflects the real world they will face after graduation.

Evergreen's learning environment can attract and produce top talent, as evidenced by some very famous alumni. Matt Groening, the creator of the Simpsons and Futurama, described Evergreen in the early 1970s as "a hippie college, with no grades or required classes, that drew every weirdo in the Northwest."[21] Michael Richards studied oriental philosophy at Evergreen before graduating and landing the role of a lifetime as Kramer on *Seinfeld*. Benjamin Haggerty won 4 awards at the 56th Grammy Awards. Better known by his stage name – Macklemore – Haggerty led a hip-hop writing workshop for incarcerated youth while earning his bachelor's degree at Evergreen.[22]

By all accounts, Evergreen State College is an exemplary institution that has lived up to its founder's lofty goals and vision for nearly 50 years. The college has won several awards for its innovative approach, outstanding master's programs, undergraduate teaching, and support for Veterans.

But there aren't many institutions that can survive the Woke Warpath. In 2017, Evergreen's campus erupted into chaos as Critical Thinkers assumed complete control of the college. They rioted, held administrators hostage, and hunted down those that dared to speak out against the revolution.

"George Bridges: Evergreen's Next President"

Before being hired at Evergreen, George Bridges was the president of Whitman College in Walla Walla, Washington. During his 10-year tenure as the head of Whitman, Bridges had increased student and faculty diversity, built more robust academic programs, and "put the college on a sounder financial footing than ever before." He had been a popular president, one who connected with students and faculty alike, striving to build relationships from the ground up, not top-down. When he was chosen to lead Evergreen State College, Bridges said that he looked "forward to learning about the college's aspirations and expectations from all members of the Evergreen community."[23]

George Bridges officially began his tenure at Evergreen on October 1st, 2015. As his first order of business, Bridges spent months interviewing students, faculty, staff, and alumni across the college. As a new leader, it was essential to assess the campus climate before making substantial changes.

Bridges shared his initial observations on January 27, 2016. In his opening remarks, he thanked his colleagues for the warm welcome and, more specifically, thanked them for "the ongoing conversations you're having about inclusion, equity, race, and ethnicity on campus." He continued, "I'm so proud of our campus that we are embracing these issues directly and energetically, and so many of us are participating in those conversations."[24]

When Bridges took charge of Evergreen, Critical Social Justice activism had entrenched itself in the mainstream political discourse in America. The premier example of this was the Black Lives Matter (BLM) organization. No longer was #BlackLivesMatter just a slogan or statement, as it technically was when Critical Thinkers popularized the Twitter hashtag in the wake of Trayvon Martin's death. BLM was now (in 2015) a national organization with dozens of chapters. Just two months before Bridges took office, one Black Lives Matter chapter in Seattle shut down a Bernie Sanders rally that had been scheduled to celebrate the anniversary of Social Security and Medicare.[25] Sanders, who was a Democratic presidential nominee at the time, opened his speech with, "Thank you Seattle for being one of the most progressive cities in the United States of America."[26] Seconds later, Marissa Janae Johnson, the co-founder of the local BLM chapter, interrupted the rally by storming the podium and screaming hysterically at the event organizers. "You are never going to hear Bernie speak if I don't hear silence now," she said. She continued, "Now that you've covered yourself in your white supremacist liberalism, I will formally welcome Bernie Sanders to Seattle."[27]

A month before Bridges assumed his new role at Evergreen, a Kentucky county clerk refused to license a couple seeking a same-sex marriage.[28] That same month, Freddie Gray's family was awarded a $6.4 million settlement by the city of Baltimore. Gray had died in April after sustaining a severe spinal cord injury while in police custody.[29] With the proliferation of smartphones and social media, it appeared that some injustice or another was being uncovered daily throughout the country. Black Americans appeared to be the most victimized. This, compounded with a ravenous news cycle preparing for a remarkable presidential election, forced social justice issues into the homes, schools, and workplaces of every person connected to the 21st century. For many Americans, it was the time to address the issues they deeply cared about, issues that appeared to be far worse than previously imaginable. The public forced politicians and institutional leaders to take strong stances, and to take radical steps to make things right. At Evergreen, the faculty would lead the charge.

On September 4th, 2015, Aisha Harrison, an art teacher at Evergreen, sent an email that would catalyze a revolution to Evergreen's all-staff and faculty distribution list. In her email, Harrison forwarded the radical claim that, as an American institution, Evergreen was rotten with systemic racism. She referenced several high-profile police shootings of black Americans in recent years, specifically citing an incident in which two black men had been shot by a white cop near her house in May of 2015. Harrison asked her coworkers to, "Imagine for a minute living in fear for your life and the lives of those you love on a daily basis." Being a new mother left Harrison feeling ashamed that she hadn't previously dared to discuss her feelings openly. "Confronting our privilege and learning to teach about racism is the least we can do," she concluded.

The responses to Harrison's "Coming Together" email chain were overwhelmingly supportive. The first response came from a faculty member who stated that, "Identifying my own White privilege and Eurocentrism has been a liberating first step."[30] Another wrote that, "If I were to post something to our email system about every single instance of casual and institutional racism on this campus that I experience, your inboxes would indeed be full of nothing but messages from me."[31] It was clear that a contingent of Evergreen faculty agreed deeply with and appreciated Harrison's email and call to action. This contingent concluded that they must do something.

It was incumbent on them to set the cogs of fundamental change in motion.

The "Coming Together Forum: A Call to Action" was held on October 28th, 2015, shortly after George Bridges began his tenure. In a recorded address, Bridges stated that this forum would have three primary goals:

1. To continue to learn about the perceptions and experiences of our students, faculty, and staff of color
2. To create and establish a series of action items that will ensure the Evergreen campus is an environment that is welcoming, safe, and supportive of traditionally underrepresented people
3. To inspire every member of the Evergreen community to participate in the programs and activities that we develop in an effort to achieve the campus climate and environment that we all seek.[32]

For those that had responded to Harrison's "Coming Together" email chain two months earlier, and for many others that had been shocked to learn about the nearly insurmountable amounts of racism at Evergreen, this forum provided both the time and place for the faculty to come together and define the scope of the systemic problems they were facing. During the forum, one attendee read from a list of "core tenets" developed by "antiracist educators."

1. Racism exists today in both traditional and modern forms.
2. Racism is an institutionalized, multilayered, multileveled system that distributes unequal power and resources between white people and people of color, as socially identified, and disproportionately benefits whites.
3. All members of society are socialized to participate in the system of racism, albeit within varied social locations.

4. All white people benefit from racism, regardless of intention.
5. No one chose to be socialized into racism, so no one is "bad," but no one is neutral. To not act against racism is to support racism.
6. Racism must be continually identified, analyzed, and challenged. No one is ever done.
7. The question is not, "Did racism take place?" but rather, "How did racism manifest in that situation?"
8. The racial status quo is comfortable for most whites. Therefore, anything that maintains white comfort is suspect.
9. The racially oppressed have a more intimate insight via experiential knowledge of the system of race than their racial oppressors. However, white professors will be seen as having more legitimacy. Thus, positionality must be intentionally engaged.[33]
10. Resistance is a predictable reaction to antiracist education and must be explicitly and strategically addressed.

Critical Thinkers developed these tenets at the Third Quadrennial Race and Pedagogy National Conference in Tacoma, Washington, in September of 2014. "What NOW is the Work of Education and Justice?: Mapping a New Critical Conscience" was organized around three primary themes: "Freedom and Civil Rights Struggles: Legacies and Invisibilities," "Institutional Readiness and Transformation," and "Revolutionary Pedagogies." In a letter to conference attendees, University of Puget Sound President Ronald R. Thomas described the United States' contemporary relationship with race as a "shameful litany of ignorance, injustice, intolerance, incarceration, and indifference."[34] Thomas's view was that educators were on the front line in the battle to develop a new critical consciousness throughout the country. Faculty and staff were to become agents of justice, tasked with understanding Critical Social Justice Theory and applying it to their institutional and educational practices.

With a handful of faculty demanding systemic change, Evergreen's administrators began inviting guest speakers to help all faculty and staff understand how dire the situation was. Faculty were surprised to learn that "all white people benefit from racism, regardless of intention" and that racism manifests itself in every situation. Critical Thinkers enlightened these confused members of faculty, helping them to understand what being an antiracist really meant.

Between January and March of 2016, Robin DiAngelo was a three-time guest speaker at "The Coming Together Speaker Series," a lecture series "focused on addressing many of the problems and challenges that face the students, faculty, and staff of color at the Evergreen State College." [35] DiAngelo was an acclaimed antiracist educator, known for her specialization in "Whiteness Studies" and "Critical Discourse Analysis." This was before she became the infamous author of 2018's *White Fragility*. In her presentations, DiAngelo argued that society is socially constructed so that racism and white supremacy are guaranteed to persist, manipulating every person within that society, even in the absence of a single racist individual. She would go on to describe the following statements as "Dominant White Racial Narratives"; "I see people as individuals," "Race doesn't' have any meaning to me," "I was taught to treat everyone the same." "Whites," she would argue, need to be "willing to tolerate the discomfort associated with an honest appraisal and discussion of your internalized superiority and racial privilege." White attendees needed to challenge their "racial reality" and "address your internalized racism."

In 2015, a disconnected patchwork of Critical Thinkers were demanding change. Now, these Critical Thinkers had a base of support and were formalizing their battle plan. They turned inward on the institution, pressuring administrators into creating concrete action plans to tackle racism. In April of 2016, six months after

Harrison's email, under the leadership of George Bridges' new administration, the Equity and Inclusion Council at Evergreen was formed.

Into the Canoe

On April 20th, 2016, in Seminar 2 B2109, "The Council" held its initial meeting.[36] The purpose was explicit; eradicate racism at Evergreen State College and create "equitable" outcomes for under-represented populations. In this sense, "equitable outcomes" meant providing all students with guaranteed equality of outcome, as opposed to equality of opportunity. The Council would recruit a Senior Equity & Diversity Officer and develop specific goals and action items for Evergreen's administration. Critical Thinkers demanded Faculty "demonstrate continued professional development or new learning about equity across race and other identities which intersect with race" and "address their learning about equity, and address equity in their teaching practices, in their annual self-evaluation."[37] In other words, The Council's charge wasn't to report on incidences of racism as they surfaced. It was to indoctrinate all faculty into practicing Critical Thinking, with the understanding that those faculty would themselves agree with and act upon The Council's goals and definitions, being responsible for reporting back on their contributions when called upon.

After months of development, The Council unveiled the 2016-2017 Strategic Equity Plan in November 2016. On November 18, nearly 300 faculty, staff, and students gathered to hear members of The Council report back on their findings and recommendations. Phyllis Esposito, one of The Council's co-chairs, set the tone of the meeting by daring the audience to look at the Strategic Equity Plan and interpret The Council's findings and data any differently than she had. Although Evergreen did "diversity" well, she said it had not yet begun tackling equity. "We're moving from a diversity agenda to an equity agenda and to do that kind of work requires painful conversation and action," she explained.[38]

George Bridges spoke at the event, calling The Council's plan "incredible." [39] According to Bridges, Evergreen hadn't been doing nearly enough to address the systemic inequities on his campus. Described as "pervasive and pernicious," these inequities were so bad that Bridges felt the need to apologize for them while speaking. On the verge of tears, he demanded that student outcomes at Evergreen improve. However, he didn't bother to list any specific evidence that disparate outcomes were being caused by institutional racism at his college.

The Council sold its plan as a series of recommendations. But, for anyone in attendance, it appeared nothing was optional. "Today, we launch a new campaign to fight the systemic causes of inequities at Evergreen," Bridges said. [40] Speaker after speaker addressed the audience as if it was a foregone conclusion that everyone was going to subscribe to the recommendations of The Council and demonstrate their fealty to the growing Critical Orthodoxy on campus. The Strategic Equity Plan was not up for debate. "Our work in pursuing these goals will never end. It will be ongoing for the future of the college," Bridges said.[41]

During this meeting, nearly all Evergreen faculty and staff saw the Strategic Equity Plan for the first time. They hadn't received the report before the meeting and, consequently, they hadn't had any time to review The Council's research, purported purpose, goals, definitions, or action items. The report was 38 pages long, and The Council expected everyone to hop on board with the radical agenda as it was unfolding. Felix Braffith, a co-chair of The Council, explained that he and his other Council members had built in time to their forum to do the "necessary work" of discussing the plan and why they were making the recommendations that they were making.[42]

Sonja Wiedenhaupt, a member of The Council, stated that "the purpose of this exercise" was to "seek to understand the goals."[43] But the purpose wasn't to question the goals, the research methodology, and the conclusions of The Council, or to open the conversation up for debating specific measures and actions. The purpose was to buckle up and accept the goals and recommendations at face value. The Council expected attendees to read the goals live, with Wiedenhaupt telling them they needed to "make sense of them."[44] The Council gave everyone only minutes to review the document. After some brief discussion, Esposito added that "Our equity goals will not be a destination. We will not ever arrive." She concluded her remarks with an ominous statement – "We are inviting you to come along. We're gonna do it. Don't get it twisted. But we would like for you to join us on this road. On this journey... If you want to be an obstructionist – work on your own!"[45]

Esposito was not mincing words, and neither was any other Council Member who spoke that day. Braffith quite literally had attendees "board" a metaphorical canoe to begin Evergreen's journey towards a more equitable future, asking those in attendance to come to the microphone and make a commitment to the Council's plans before "boarding." A line quickly formed, with many staff and faculty taking turns declaring their allegiance to the new, formalized Critical Orthodoxy on campus. This meeting, "The Equity Canoe Event," would tip the scales of power at Evergreen, setting in motion a series of catastrophic events for the college. In The Evergreen State College Production's video of that meeting, at the 1:30:13 mark, as those on the canoe exited the room to the sound of Native American drums, Bret Weinstein can be seen standing in disbelief.

A Day of Absence

Each year, Evergreen State College celebrates a two-day event for faculty, staff, and students to explore issues of race, equity, allyship, inclusion, and privilege.[46] On the first day of the event, the Day of Absence (DOA), students, faculty, and staff of color at Evergreen absent themselves from campus, meeting elsewhere to attend various workshops and events to discuss their experiences as people of color on campus and, more broadly, society at large. The reasoning used to justify this segregation is this – people of color are integral to the success of the college, and, without their presence, white people can truly learn to appreciate the contributions of historically marginalized groups by physically feeling the lack of said contributions for a full day. The second day of the event, the Day of Presence (DOP), sees everyone reunited to have group discussions about racism, power, and privilege.

Since the 1970s, the Day of Absence and Day of Presence has followed the same format. This changed in 2017 as Evergreen's new equity regime reimagined what social justice looks like. The Cooper Point Journal, Evergreen's student newspaper, reported on April 10th, 2017 that, "This year, however, it was decided that on Day of Absence, white students, staff and faculty will be invited to leave the campus for the day's activities. This decision was reached through discussion with POC Greeners who voiced concern over feeling as if they are unwelcome on campus, following the 2016 election."[47] DOA and DOP would take place on April 12th and April 14th in 2017.

This announcement was shared nearly a month earlier, on March 14th, in an email sent to Evergreen's All Staff & Faculty Distribution List by Rashida Love, Evergreen's Director of First Peoples Multicultural Advising Services. "By committing to participate in DOA/DOP," she wrote, "you are engaging in an innovative and unique opportunity to examine equity and difference in an academic environment that truly exemplifies Evergreen's commitment to learning across significant differences."[48]

A day after Rashida Love made the announcement, she received a reply from biology faculty member Bret Weinstein. In his response, Weinstein wrote that;

> There is a huge difference between a group or coalition deciding to voluntarily absent themselves from a shared space in order to

> highlight their vital and under-appreciated roles (The theme of the Douglas Turner Ward play *Day of Absence*, as well as the recent Women's Day walkout), and a group or coalition encouraging another group to go away. The first is a forceful call to consciousness which is, of course, crippling to the logic of oppression. The second is a show of force, and an act of oppression in and of itself.
>
> You may take this letter as a formal protest of this year's structure, and you may assume I will be on campus on the Day of Absence. I would encourage others to put phenotype aside and reject this new formulation, whether they have 'registered' for it already or not. On a college campus, one's right to speak – or to be – must never be based on skin color.[49]

So, Weinstein was on campus on the day on which white faculty, staff, and students had been asked to leave. For those welcome on campus, several workshops, seminars, and discussions took place. In *Building Safety Outside The System: How to Cultivate Liberatory Relationships and Deal With Harm in Transformational Ways*, participants learned how to "build concrete skills to engage with ourselves and others to transform the conditions that allow violence to happen." In *Identifying Anti-Blackness in Yourself and Your Intimate and Sexual Relationships*, participants sought "to explore, discuss and strategize action against the propagation of anti-blackness within our sexual and intimate relationships." In *101 on Race and Micro-aggressions: How White Supremacy Invalidates Us*, attendees would "discuss how creating academic terms for racism is a tool of white supremacy." And, in *How Asian-Americans Contribute to White Supremacy*, attendees would "work to understand the model minority construct as well as the cultural, economic, and political ways AAs aid white supremacy and derail justice in this country."[50]

Weinstein's formal protest of 2017's DOA went seemingly unnoticed. That is, until dozens of students had decided enough was enough. Bret Weinstein's objection to the DOA was incomprehensibly racist and would not be tolerated. These students subsequently cornered Weinstein outside of his classroom on May 23rd, chanting, "Hey, hey, ho, ho, Bret Weinstein has got to go."[51]

Protests and Riots

Weinstein tried to reason with the students, many of whom called him a racist and demanded he resign. But they would have none of that. "Listen! You're going to listen," shouted one protestor. "This is not a discussion. You lost that one! You said racist shit! Now apologize!" demanded another.[52] Weinstein's email correspondence to Rashida Love had leaked, and students were enraged that a white faculty member could be allowed to exit the canoe. Weinstein offered to have a civil conversation about his stance on the issue, stating that he believed in equity but felt this was the absolute worst way to go about it. The students were not interested in such a conversation. They wanted Weinstein to bend the knee.

Campus administrators called the police to ensure this campus protest didn't end in violence. Upon seeing officers, one of Weinstein's protestors encouraged white students to form a barrier between the police and black students, presumably because that protestor believed that all cops were racist murderers. "White people! White people! White people!"[53] she shouted. In a video of the event, another protestor calls one officer a "fucking pig."[54]

Weinstein escaped to safety, but the protest had only just begun. George Bridges and senior campus administrators granted an audience to protest leaders to discuss why things had escalated so quickly. The administration wanted to know what was going on and how they could help. "We deliberately asked white students to be a barrier between the police because we know the relationship that black and brown people have with the police," said one protestor.

Another said, "So I want you to really sit with that when you go home and kiss your white kids. Remember that you did that to us. You stuck us out in the cold [by calling the cops]. Your silence is white violence."[55]

George Bridges and the other administrators had spent months inviting Critical Thinkers to take over the college, by creating a Diversity, Equity, and Inclusion regime (The Council) that would force the widespread acceptance of a Critical Orthodoxy on campus. Now they would suffer the consequences.

In speaking to the student protestors who had just accused his administration of "white violence," Bridges said he believed in the equity plan and understood that Bret Weinstein's emails were racist. Demonstrating his allegiance to their cause, Bridges told the students, "The problem is, a problem, they have an opportunity to speak their mind even if sometimes they do it in the most offensive ways, and how do we stop people from speaking offensively? That's a challenge. There is this concept of free speech."[56]

The protestors didn't like that answer. They accused the campus administration of upholding a racist system and demanded action. Bridges, wholly stripped of moral authority, capitulated to the protestors, laying out a working plan to move forward. "They're going to say some things we don't like, and it's our job to bring them all in or get them all out. Bring 'em in, train 'em, and if they don't get it, sanction them. I want you to hold me to that."

Later that day, hundreds of protestors gathered in the campus cafeteria to air their grievances as George Bridges desperately tried to ease tensions. But that had become an impossible task. The supply of grievance had grown beyond anyone's ability to contain it.

"That's how whiteness works. Whiteness is the most violent fuckin' system ever to breathe!" said one protestor. "You know what changes shit? Action. That's why the fuck we in this room," said another.

Bridges was mocked, belittled, and silenced. Protestors wouldn't allow him to use hand gestures when speaking, and they certainly weren't going to let him walk away without committing to doing whatever it was they wanted him to do. Feeling the enormous pressure to conform to the dictates of the monster he had created, Bridges capitulated yet again, saying, "I will commit. I will commit to dealing with my own shit. My own racism."[57]

In granting the protestors the moral authority to justify their actions, George Bridges had handed radicals the campus keys. The next day, protestors turned riotous, barricading campus buildings to keep students, administrators, and faculty in, while keeping police out. Bridges and other power players were locked in a room and forced to commit to a conversation about student demands. These included: campus funded healthcare at no cost to students; no expansion of police facilities or services at any point in time; mandatory sensitivity and cultural competency training for all staff, administrators, and student employees; the creation of an Equity Center; and the immediate suspension of Bret Weinstein without pay.[58]

It's difficult to put into words the insanity of the situation. During the "meeting" in which rioters made their demands, Bridges indicated that he needed to pee. Rioters told him to "hold it" and locked him in a room. Rioters then assigned students to track the movements and actions of campus administrators. No action was to be taken, nor an utterance made, without the mob's consent.

Rioters would also coerce students and faculty to stay on campus and join the revolution. "By leaving, you're sort of showing the school that you don't care about the black and brown lives here, and that's harmful to the environment here,"[59] said one rioter to a terrified faculty member. Anyone who tried to leave was approached and coerced in this way. As Bret Weinstein's wife, Heather Heying, would later say, the situation was "full *Lord of the Flies*."[60]

Hostages were forced to remain silent, allowed to speak only in the act of swearing allegiance and fealty to the new regime. In speaking of the events years later, Weinstein noted that one of the worst aspects of this hostile takeover was seeing his fellow faculty externalize their fear by harming other faculty to distract attention away from themselves. These members of faculty virtue signaled their hearts out. Only through self-deprecation and renunciation of one's thoughts and liberties could their original sin be tolerated, albeit not forgiven.

The riots continued for days. At one point, Weinstein received a call from the police chief telling him not to come to campus because protestors were stopping traffic and hunting for him. The police chief told Weinstein that the police had barricaded themselves in their precinct and would not be able to protect him should the rioters find out where he was. The Bridge's administration had told the chief to stand down.

Dismantled

Critical Thinkers dismantled Evergreen State College in 2016 and 2017. They poisoned the telos of Evergreen, corrupting its purpose and creating a new cultural hegemony to replace the liberal and enlightenment values that once made the college great. Today, Evergreen is a hollow shell of its former self. Enrollments have tanked, George Bridges is gone, and the institution cannot find a permanent president willing to steer the ship. Critical Thinkers are running the show.

Evergreen has abdicated its mission to provide a liberal education to those who want it. It is no longer an institution of free inquiry, debate, and truth. It is a Critical Thinker's paradise, an environment built to censor and eliminate anything that would challenge the new Critical Orthodoxy. If students, faculty, or administrators step out of line, Critical Thinkers train them to overcome their false consciousness. If they "don't get it," they are sanctioned, harassed, and eliminated.

If it weren't for the summer recess of 2017, who knows how dangerous the situation would have become. If Bret Weinstein hadn't heeded the warning of the chief of police, who knows what students would have done to him. But, as dangerous as the situation was, it wasn't the riots that did the most damage to Evergreen. The real dismantling happened at the level of consciousness. Critical Thinkers convinced faculty, administrators, and students alike that their conspiratorial claims were true. They convinced good, moral people to become foot soldiers, marching on the Woke Warpath through all of America's institutions.

After Evergreen collapsed, Bret Weinstein warned the world that what had happened at his campus wasn't just "woke kids" taking things too far. It wasn't really about college campuses, free speech, or racism at all. It wasn't something that was going to go away on its own. Weinstein warned the world that what had happened at Evergreen would find its way into everything, if we're not careful.

"These ideas were wrong when they first took hold in the academy. Instead of shutting them down, we created phony fields that act as a kind of analytical affirmative action where ideas that don't deserve to survive are given sustenance. These ideas are so toxic and so ill-conceived that, to the extent that they are allowed to hold sway as if one truth is equal to every other truth – my truth is good as your truth – the extent that that idea is allowed to pervade other institutions on which civilizations depends, civilization will come apart. We have to fight this."[61]

Bret Weinstein understood that Critical Thinkers are not at all concerned with social justice. They are only concerned with power. Critical Social Justice movements are nothing more than mechanisms to steal power and force everyone to break society and bring about the revolution. Critical Thinkers coerce people to live in a fantasy world where racism is OK if the right people suffer from it, where only a select few are allowed to speak, group identity is sacred, equity suffocates equality, and freedom is too great a burden to bear.

No "system" was oppressing the students at Evergreen in 2016 and 2017. Those students were, objectively, among the most privileged humans ever to have lived, as are all students attending university in the United States. The poisonous influence of Critical

Thinkers led these kids to mental illness, anxiety, and depression, just as Marcuse prescribed in the 1960s and 70s. The point of disrupting and dismantling isn't to break material things, although that certainly does happen. The point is to disrupt normal human cognition, tricking the brain into thinking that it sees things that aren't there. Panicked, the mind primes itself to adopt a worldview that can explain the chaotic situation it now finds itself in. Convincing a person that they are the subject of ever-present oppression makes them a victim without agency and control. Giving that person the postmodern neo-Marxist toolkit to sort it all out stabilizes a problem that never existed in the first place. This abuse is a form of emotional manipulation of which only psychopaths are capable.

The dismantling of the mind has disastrous consequences. People that have developed a Critical Consciousness begin supporting and advocating for illiberal causes, and supporting racist and sexist policies in the name of "progress." At Evergreen, Critical Thinkers told a white faculty member not to be on campus because of his skin color. Even a cursory reading of history should be enough to know what terrible atrocities have been justified by people who think in this way.

CHAPTER THREE

BATTLEPLAN: DISRUPT AND DISMANTLE

> The whole system of oppression ... was based on keeping malcontents apart, preventing them from reading each other's eyes and discovering how many of them there were; instilling it into all of them, even into the most dissatisfied, that no one was dissatisfied except for a few doomed individuals, blindly vicious and spiritually bankrupt.
>
> –Aleksandr Solzhenitsyn,
> *The Gulag Archipelago*

The collapse of Evergreen State College should have been a national wake-up call. A group of radicals had captured an institution in months, and within a year, they had effectively dismantled it. Bret Weinstein sounded the alarm – something insidious was happening on college campuses, and it would be in everyone's best interest to figure out exactly what that thing was.

But the speed at which Evergreen had fallen would become the very reason to discredit Weinstein's voice. The events at Evergreen were too outrageous to be believed. Americans had seen campus activism before, and this was treated as just a case of students taking things too far. Popular media outlets like CNN boiled the affair down to a single line – "Some students demanded that Weinstein be fired and angrily confronted him."[62]

In reality, the Evergreen meltdown wasn't "students taking things too far." It was precisely what one would expect to happen when Critical Thinkers are allowed to disrupt and dismantle everything.

Critical Thinkers captured Evergreen by using radical claims to disrupt the college's systems of governance. They accused Evergreen administrators of upholding systems of oppression. With their new moral authority, Critical Thinkers demanded the power to begin dismantling Evergreen in accordance with their various postmodern and critical theories. Most ignored Bret Weinstein's alarm in 2017. In 2022, we are reeling from the effects of Gramsci's prescribed "long march through the institutions." We are Evergreen at the national level.

Today, Critical Thinkers across the country are introducing radical claims into our workplaces, schools, and systems of governance to secure power and begin dismantling everything. They achieve this by stealing the moral high ground, forcing people to have conversations on their terms, and implementing authoritarian Diversity, Equity, and Inclusion regimes to cement their power and cast out any would-be troublemakers.

STAGE 1: Radical Claims

Critical Thinkers believe that the fundamental organizing principle of society is power: the power of the rich over the poor; the power of men over women; the power of whites over blacks; the power of oppressors over the oppressed. As they think in this way, they are utterly uninterested in anything that doesn't involve securing more power. This is their primary goal.

Their secondary goal is to change something. Specifically, Critical Thinkers seek to critique something and demonstrate all of the ways in which that thing doesn't align with postmodern neo-Marxist Critical Theory. They arrest power with a radical critique to begin the disrupt and dismantle process.

However, power is hard to come by. Western liberal democracies aren't organized by power hierarchies. They are overwhelmingly organized by competence hierarchies. Generally, society gives power to competent people. Free market economies incentivize workers to build higher levels of competence to secure higher wages and better benefits. Society rewards the best surgeons for the incredible levels of competence they bring into the operating room. Their skills and years of experience are demonstrable. It would be immediately evident if a surgeon didn't command high levels of competence – their surgeries would be unsuccessful, and they wouldn't be a surgeon for long. The same goes for electricians, professional athletes, lawyers, and business owners. In general, the more competence one has, the higher they rise on the competence ladder in whatever pursuit they are involved in. This is a very good thing. We want the most competent people in charge of the things that matter most.

But Critical Thinkers don't care about competence. They believe everyone is in the position they are in because of a set of preconditions that sorts society into those who are allowed to have power and those who are not. To change things, they need to convince those with high levels of competence that there is something radically wrong with the way things are being done. They need to convert critical thinkers into Critical Thinkers.

Critical Thinkers do this by making radical claims. A Chief Human Resources Officer (CHRO) is unlikely to hand over the keys to someone demanding the power to radically restructure ABC

Company. A better strategy is to tell that Chief Human Resources Officer that you think their company is sexist and racist. This is the tried-and-tested method of a Critical Thinker.

A competent CHRO is likely to ask for evidence of such accusations. The Critical Thinker offers evidence that women hold only 45 percent of managerial positions. Not only that, but the company has only onboarded one black man out of the last two rounds of hiring. The company has hired no black women or LGBTQ (lesbian, gay, bisexual, trans, queer) identifying people into managerial roles. The Critical Thinker uses these claims to create an inescapable trap for the CHRO.

There can be a perfectly reasonable explanation for each of these disparities. It could be that 45 percent of the company's employees are women, and thus only 45 percent of those in managerial roles are women. It could be that only one black man applied in the last two rounds of hiring. It could also be that there are no black women that work for the company, and it is either impossible to know or unethical to share whether or not anyone in a managerial role is LGBT or Q. For each of these responses, the Critical Thinker has their counter reply.

"Women are 50 percent of the population. Why is the company not hiring more women?"

"Why is the company doing so little to attract black male applicants?"

"Why is it that not a single black woman works for this company?"

"Why have you created a culture so exclusive that LGBTQ peoples do not feel safe in openly expressing their gender identities in the workplace?"

These counter-arguments reinforce the original radical claim that ABC Company is sexist and racist. It doesn't matter what the CHRO says – the Critical Thinker will always find a disparity and assume discrimination is at play. Critical Thinkers believe human beings have infinitely divisible, socially constructed identities, and it is impossible not to have a disparity to draw from. The Critical Thinker is begging the CHRO to avoid playing the game.

This type of radical claim achieves two things. First, it places the Critical Thinker on the moral high ground. The CHRO knows that racism and sexism are bad things and does not want to be associated with those accusations. Secondly, it places the CHRO on the defensive, asking them to explain incredibly complex, multivariate, and perhaps unknowable things. There may be a thousand reasons why these disparities exist, and asking the CHRO to become personally responsible for each explanation is an impossible task to overcome. Besides, the Critical Thinker won't accept a single explanation that doesn't involve discrimination. That is how they understand the world.

At Evergreen, Aisha Harrison forwarded the radical claim that the college was radically racist and sexist. The Critical Thinkers who joined her leveled the same charge and would not allow an honest discussion in dispute of the claim. The Equity Council used student demographic data as evidence that the college was exclusionary. The student body was not representative of the U.S. population at large. According to Harrison and others, this was proof that discrimination was taking place.

After introducing the radical claim, taking the moral high ground, and putting the CHRO on the defensive, the Critical Thinker makes their next move. They demand that the CHRO must explore these issues, including the Critical Thinker in that exploration process. At this stage, the goal of the Critical Thinker is to trick the organization into affording legitimacy to radical claims. The Critical Thinker needs an open door for their postmodern neo-Marxist Trojan Horse.

STAGE 2: Offer False Choices to Build Your Base

A radical claim doesn't have to involve accusing a person or institution of being racist or sexist (although this is the preferred method). It can also include a critique of what institutions produce, don't produce, and support, or don't support. For instance, Critical Thinkers accused Johnson & Johnson of producing a product that wasn't sufficiently inclusive – band-aids. The company took to Instagram to post;

"We hear you. We see you. We're listening to you. We stand in solidarity with our Black colleagues, collaborators and community in the fight against racism, violence and injustice. We are committed to taking actions to create tangible change for the Black community."[63]

Different colored bandages aren't a problem. The fact that Critical Thinkers have captured one of the most powerful pharmaceutical companies on the planet is. In November 2020, the company announced a 100 million dollar commitment to "promote health equity solutions for Black people and other communities of color." According to a statement, "Society has been significantly impacted by systemic racism," which has "spotlighted healthcare inequities."[64] In this context, "health equity" means providing healthcare treatments to people based on skin color. It means handing over our healthcare administrations to Critical Thinkers who are charged with determining who gets access and preferential treatment.

To capture a company as large as Johnson & Johnson, Critical Thinkers must mount radical claims and force an organizational conversation about sexism and racism on the Critical Thinker's terms. To do this, Critical Thinkers must first build their base of support by finding their allies and collectively demanding that their radical claims be addressed immediately. They must flood the door they opened in Stage 1 with more Critical Thinkers. Dealing with one person leveling false accusations of racism and sexism is a somewhat manageable problem. Coping with a handful of radicals is a different story altogether.

The first step in the coalition-building process is to create a false dichotomy and then use it as a tool to coerce others to begin thinking Critically. A false dichotomy is a logical fallacy wherein two opposing options are presented as the only possible choices available. In a typical false dichotomy, one of the options is entirely off the table. You really don't have a choice; it has already been made for you by limiting the options to two things – one "bad" and one "good."

The most potent false dichotomy used by Critical Thinkers is the claim that one is either a racist or one is an antiracist.

"The opposite of racist isn't 'not racist.' It is 'antiracist.' What's the difference? One endorses either the idea of a racial hierarchy as a racist, or racial equality as an antiracist. One either believes problems are rooted in groups of people, as a racist, or locates the roots of problems in power and policies, as an antiracist. One either allows racial inequities to persevere, as a racist, or confronts racial inequities, as an antiracist. There is no in-between safe space of 'not racist.'" – *Ibram X. Kendi, How to be an Antiracist*

The simplicity of this false dichotomy gives it a terrible strength. When a Critical Thinker asks someone whether they are a racist or an antiracist, it is clear that there is only one option. However, this is a false choice. By eliminating the "not racist" option, the Critical Thinker forces people to buy into whatever they have defined "antiracist" to mean – and it certainly does not mean "not racist." No longer can someone simply acknowledge that racism is bad or that they are against it. They are forced to accept the Critical Thinker's terms and begin playing the game of Critical Thinking.

Racism is usually defined as the belief that race determines human traits and abilities and that racial differences produce inherent superiority or inferiority in humans.[65] But that is not the definition used by Critical Thinkers. Critical Thinkers define racism in "systemic" terms. They believe that there is systemic racism, meaning that racism is built into the foundation of Western liberal democracies. This racism expresses itself as power differentials between privileged and oppressed groups.

Critical Thinkers believe that straight, white, European men have corrupted every institution, codifying racism in written and unwritten ways into all aspects of society. Critical Thinkers argue that they must disrupt and dismantle everything to "reimagine" this system and liberate oppressed people. We could live in a world free of a single racist person and this wouldn't change a thing. According to Critical Thinkers, the system itself reproduces these racial power differentials and must be dismantled. This takes us back to the quote from Robin DiAngelo – "The question is not, "Did racism take place"? but "How did racism manifest in that situation?"[66]

According to the world's leading antiracist, Ibram X. Kendi, to be an antiracist one must be against racist policies. Again, the Critical Thinker offers a false dichotomy. You are either for "racist policies" or against "racist policies." There is no third option to choose from. Every policy must either be racist or antiracist.

Kendi defines a racist policy as "any measure that produces or sustains racial inequity between racial groups. By policy, I mean written and unwritten laws, rules, procedures, processes, regulations, and guidelines that govern people."[67] Thus, if we are to follow Kendi's definition, we are to look for any policy that results in a disparity between various groups and assume that this disparity is the result of racism. There is no room to explore the disparity from an objective place, using traditional theories to try and understand why some people – for various political, economic, or cultural reasons – choose to do certain things and act in certain ways. No policies are neutral.

There is no "in-between safe space" to run to – and this is by design. By redefining common words and using new definitions interchangeably with the old, the Critical Thinker can confuse people into accepting their terms of engagement. "You are either with me as an antiracist or you are a racist (or anti-sexist or anti-anything the Critical Thinker wants to play this game with)." The Critical Thinker uses this tactic to have "critical and courageous conversations" around the workplace, asking everyone to join them in the fight for social justice. Even those disinterested in having socio-political conversations at work are forced to choose a side. No one wants to be labeled the "person who goes quiet" whenever Critical Thinkers discuss racism. No one wants to be the person who says, "Yeah, but...."

The second step in the coalition-building process is to coalesce the recently converted Critical Thinkers and turn them inwards on the institution. At this stage, Critical Thinkers begin to demand time on the agenda to discuss race, sex, and gender. They pressure key decision-makers with false choices and begin to tie the disparities seen in their organization with society at large. They begin to accuse leaders in the organization of allowing the business to reproduce systems of oppression by continuing to support this policy or that. In short, Critical Thinkers take their base of support and begin to disrupt the entire operation. They force their way into conversations and positions of influence by making ever more radical claims and offering ever more radical choices.

This stage happens incredibly quickly. Once accusations of racism and sexism begin flying around, people take notice. No one likes to be accused of being a sexist or a racist when they are not. No one wants to be charged with supporting sexist or racist things – people distance themselves. This disruption scrambles the higher faculties of the brain. Luckily, the Critical Thinker always offers the organization a way out.

"You may not have known that we live in a systemically racist society. You may not have understood that the organization is upholding these systems of oppression. But now you're educated and I'm offering you a choice to support antiracism; to acknowledge your privileged position and become an ally. It's OK, and you have a way out."

At Evergreen, Critical Thinkers used their radical claims to build a base of support in George Bridge's administration. They forced a conversation on their terms and demanded action. When they were given formal governing authority in The Equity Council, they secured the power to force other faculty and staff to begin playing their game.

STAGE 3: Diversity, Equity, Inclusion

The dismantling process has begun. At this stage, the Critical Thinker has introduced a radical claim that has disrupted their organization. They have used this initial disruption to build their base of support and force people to have conversations about race, sex, and gender on their terms.

The Critical Thinker's next goal is to demand commitments and develop new rules and ways of talking about things. The Critical Thinker aims to foster an environment where everyone is compelled to think Critically.

This can be difficult if too many people oppose the changes they want to make. To get everyone on board, the Critical Thinker must use their new influence to convince leadership to develop a framework from which the organization can reorient itself and begin the "healing process". That is to say, the Critical Thinker must create new mechanisms of control to police the thoughts and actions of workers. No one can be allowed to impede "social justice." To achieve this end, the Critical Thinker uses Diversity, Equity, and Inclusion (DEI).

Critical Thinkers use DEI frameworks to dismantle the very things for which they purport to stand. Like radical claims, Diversity, Equity, and Inclusion commitments are a woke Trojan Horse. Once inside, DEI corrupts the everyday language people use to discuss race, sex, gender, and workplace culture. With DEI, Critical Thinkers trick well-intentioned and moral people into investing in an illiberal machine that will grant Critical Thinkers the organizational power they lust for.

Diversity

Critical Thinkers advocate for diversity of thought, perspective, and opinion in a very deceptive way. If employees are allowed to express their disagreement with the organization's direction, other employees may feel free or obligated to do so. Allowing real diversity of thought and opinion threatens to put the brakes on all of the dismantling that Critical Thinkers want to do.

In the eyes of a Critical Thinker, valuing diversity only means valuing the thoughts and opinions of other trained Critical Thinkers. It means propping up various identity categories (as defined by critical and postmodern theories) because those categories have a unique knowledge afforded to them by the ways in which their identities intersect with various systems of power.[68] In other words, those groups deemed to be marginalized by systemic racism and sexism have a special knowledge – a lived experience – that gives them a unique voice to talk about how sexism and racism works. Only those with a sufficiently developed critical consciousness are considered to have "diverse" viewpoints, even though they think alike.

To illustrate how different the Critical Thinker's "diversity" is, consider the definition of diversity provided by Critical Thinkers at Queensborough Community College in NY.

"Diversity is a set of conscious practices that involve… understanding that diversity includes not only ways of being but also ways of knowing."[69]

For the Critical Thinker, a "way of knowing" refers to "experience, confessions, and testimony" as "vital dimensions of any learning process."[70] That is to say, "diversifying" a space is the practice of placing those with a critical consciousness in power to tell everyone else how awful their differences are; it is the practice of allowing trained Critical Thinkers to use anecdotal evidence to force others to conform to an identical view of the world.

By framing diversity in this way, Critical Thinkers level viewpoint diversity to inculcate employees into groupthink. Determining whether or not an organization is diverse enough no longer involves an assessment of the richness of viewpoints within that organization. To achieve Critical Diversity, an organization must seek to hire and prop up only those employees who think and act according to the dictates of Critical Thinkers. It doesn't matter if an employee is white, black, or brown – if they don't think in the ways expected of them, the Critical Thinker opposes the kind of diversity they bring to the table. This is the reason why, during his campaign to replace Gavin Newsome as California's governor in 2021, Larry Elder, a black man, was called "the black face of white supremacy."[71] Elder didn't think or act in the way Critical Thinkers expected him to. He wasn't "authentically black" because he rejected the idea of placing social significance into racial categories to achieve power.

Equity

Equity is very different from equality. Whereas a traditional diversity program highlights the importance of equality of opportunity and fairness, a DEI program advocates for equality of outcome. Equity is the redistribution of opportunity, resources, and privilege until everyone is made equal in whatever endeavor they need to be made equal in.

For example, the United Way of the National Capital Area in Washington, DC, defines equity this way;

"Equity, in its simplest terms as it relates to racial and social justice, means meeting communities where they are and allocating resources and opportunities as needed to create equal outcomes for all community members."[72]

For the Critical Thinker, advocating for equality of opportunity is something oppressive systems do to camouflage the power imbalances innate to those systems. "Equality of opportunity" is a slogan used by those with privilege and power to justify why they are in the position they are in; to argue, "We all had an equal shot at getting here and I took mine!"

Critical Thinkers argue that Western liberal democracies are not providing and have never provided equal opportunity. A person's various, unique intersecting identities determine how systems of oppression treat them. Therefore, disparities in outcome between peoples are not attributed to things like work ethic, personal decision making, random chance, actual discrimination, poverty, or merit; they are attributed to a system that provides unequal access to privilege and power. Whenever there is a disparate outcome between two groups, it is assumed that society is not treating the lagging group fairly. They are not getting the access they need to satisfy the necessary preconditions of success.

Critical Thinkers demand the power to redistribute resources, privilege, opportunity, and authority to redress these imbalances. Critical Thinkers demand the authority to decide who to hire or promote, who to place in charge of budgets and special projects, who is deemed an authority figure, and who must bear the responsibility for a company's antiracism efforts. Under equity frameworks, Critical Thinkers can doggedly remove freedoms from all individuals at will until they achieve their desired outcomes.

Inclusion

An inclusive environment is generally understood as one in which all people and ideas are welcome. This is a very good thing. However, this is not what Critical Thinkers advocate for when they use the term "inclusion."

In DEI programs, creating an "inclusive" environment means excluding anyone whose ideas or beliefs do not align with those of Critical Thinkers. Inclusive environments are meant to be "safe spaces" where "violent" thoughts cannot enter into the discourse.

Critical Thinkers believe that words and ideas – those said and even unsaid (silence is violence) – can literally cause physical harm and trauma in the bodies of oppressed identity groups. For instance, if someone were to use stock photos that depicted only heterosexual couples in a marketing meeting, those photos could make an LGBTQ co-worker feel excluded. The presenter who chose those photos was "centering heterosexuality" and eliminating a "way of being" in the world. The presenter was committing a micro-aggression that reinforced the dominant, systemic power structure of heterosexuality; they were "normalizing" heterosexuality.

Any idea, action, or statement that opposes a postmodern neo-Marxist Critical Theory can be said to generate these types of reactions. Therefore, to create a truly inclusive environment, Critical Thinkers develop new rules and speech codes to avoid such offenses. The result is that anyone who disagrees with or is indifferent regarding a specific idea or action is forced to accept the Critical Thinker's worldview. Any utterance deemed to be in opposition of the Critical Orthodoxy is by default the reproduction of oppression. Critical Thinkers don't tolerate these offenses in "inclusive" spaces.

STAGE 4: The New Regime

Critical Thinkers capture institutional power with Diversity, Equity, and Inclusion commitments. They use Critical Diversity to establish an operational system wherein individuals, teams, and committees are judged not by how many diverse ideas they produce but by how many Critical Thinkers are in their ranks. They use equity to redistribute power to those teams and committees they consider deserving of it. Finally, with competence replaced as the determining factor for who gets to make decisions and who doesn't, Critical Thinkers rewrite rules, policies, and practices to exclude any speech or thought they have deemed intolerable. Safe spaces and speech codes are used as justification to oust anyone who would challenge the new Critical Orthodoxy.

At this point, employees may be catching on to the fact that the terms "diversity, equity, and inclusion" do not mean what they thought they meant. Racism and sexism are no longer acts that someone can put their finger on; they are phantom forces only discernable to those of the new regime. Suddenly everyone is expected to "do the work" as prescribed by the political enforcers of Diversity, Equity, and Inclusion offices. Every discussion is intentionally political, and the purpose is to disrupt and dismantle the system to change it. Many employees may realize they were lied to, and morally and emotionally coerced into buying into something much larger than they bargained for. But it is too late.

Critical Thinkers look to use their new organizational power to disrupt and dismantle larger societal systems. Critical Thinkers are a virus; they capture individual organizations and use their authority to influence and infect others. Entire institutions are gobbled up in short order and used as pawns to manipulate and take over any space the Critical Thinker can get their hands on.

In the last 60 years, Critical Thinkers have infiltrated and corrupted countless organizations. They now control the institutions that influence and affect each of our daily lives; the media, the university system, the healthcare industry, K-12 education, systems of local governance, law enforcement, and more.

It would be impossible to articulate just how much damage has been done by Critical Thinkers in a single book. For that reason, I have chosen to focus the following chapters on the three things that have been broken most by the disrupt and dismantle process; policing, education, and women's rights.

The radical claims used to capture the institutional power necessary to disrupt and dismantle these institutions are as follows:

1. Racist cops casually murder unarmed black Americans.
2. Institutional and systemic racism in American education causes the black- white achievement gap.
3. We live in a patriarchy that denies women jobs and equal pay.

Critical Thinkers use radical claims to get into positions of power and influence. In the following chapters, I will focus on dismantling these radical claims to demonstrate that the critiques Critical Thinkers have leveled against society are based not on fact but a lust for power and control. I will then describe how Critical Thinkers use their control of these institutions to radically change how we police our streets, educate our children, and determine what the truth is. Prepare for a wild ride.

CHAPTER FOUR

POLICING

"We forget everything. What we remember is not what actually happened, not history, but merely that hackneyed dotted line they have chosen to drive into our memories by incessant hammering."

–Aleksandr Solzhenitsyn,
The Gulag Archipelago

On August 9th, 2014, an 18-year-old black teenager – Michael Brown – was shot and killed by a white police officer – Darren Wilson – on Canfield Drive in Ferguson, Missouri. At a news conference the next day, St. Louis County police Chief Joe Belmar detailed a situation in which the teenager had assaulted the police officer in the officer's cruiser, attempted to gain control of the officer's weapon, and been shot and killed shortly thereafter.

Eyewitness accounts of the shooting varied considerably. Two competing narratives emerged, one of which aligned with the chain of events as detailed by Chief Belmar, and another in which Michael Brown had attempted to run away, stopped, put his hands in the air, and tried to surrender before being killed.[73] One eyewitness, a close friend of Brown, had this to say;

"I seen them shoot Michael Brown in the head as soon as the police officer exited his truck... I seen my best friend in the middle of the street with his hands in the air and he said, 'please don't shoot me.' The officer got out of his car and shot him... I seen him exit his car, shoot him in his head and then he shot him eight more times. It was four gunshots, and then there was a ten second pause, and then four more... point blank range, like close... like a step away... I would never lie. I wouldn't lie on my best friend"[74]

For those who subscribed to this gut-wrenching testimony, believing Brown was attempting to surrender before being killed, Officer Darren Wilson's actions were tantamount to a state-sanctioned execution. Brown's death was yet another indication that police officers in America did not value black lives in the same way that they valued others. So, emboldened by systems upholding their racial rage, officers now felt comfortable killing teenagers in broad daylight because of the color of their skin. This shooting was not indicative of a singular racially motivated incident – it was yet another blister formed at skin level, revealing the root sickness underneath.

Peaceful candlelight vigils gave way to egregious levels of rioting and destruction in the days following the death of Michael Brown. President Barack Obama addressed the nation on August 14th, acknowledging the raw emotion so many were feeling, while at the same time saying that "there is never an excuse for violence against police, or for those that would use this tragedy for vandalism or looting."[75] For those doing the looting and rioting, this message fell on deaf ears, as it often does. On August 16th, Governor Jay Nixon declared a state of emergency, and just two days later, the National Guard was deployed.[76]

In the months following the death of Michael Brown, anger, frustration, and despair gave way to guttural anxiety. For those who believed Officer Wilson to be a vile racist whose officer's uniform empowered him to act upon his racial animosity, culminating in the execution of another black boy, the grand jury's investigation into the incident was developing into a watershed moment. Either America would finally be able to see these incidents for what they really were – vile, intentional acts of racially motivated murder – or this would be yet another case destined to be swept under the rug like so many other acts lost to our nation's collective racial amnesia.

On November 24th, St. Louis County prosecuting attorney Robert McCulloch would see that this anxiety was not misplaced. He announced that there would be no indictment of Officer Wilson for any crime related to the death of Michael Brown. It just so happens that 9 of the 12 jurors were white, which left a considerable number of Americans wondering whether the color of one's skin weighed differently on our color-blind scales of justice. One of those Americans was Michael Brown's stepfather, immortalized on video as he screamed, "Burn this bitch down!" repeatedly after hearing the news. CNN and other networks were sure to broadcast this message far and wide. The excerpt below paints a grim picture of the events that would follow that night;

"A row of businesses on West Florissant Avenue, a major thoroughfare in the St. Louis suburb, was engulfed in flames Monday night. Police cars and vehicles at a nearby dealership were turned into fireballs. There were so many blazes that firefighters couldn't reach every one."[77]

During the Ferguson riots, the Federal Aviation Administration had to divert aircraft because they feared that bullets fired into the sky by rioters posed a danger to flight crews and passengers. Local hospitals began admitting patients who had suffered head wounds and trauma from the types of things that tend to happen when thousands of people are looting and rioting. Police officers and rioters traded aerial weapons in the form of batteries, bricks, and tear gas. Protesters in Oakland, New York City, Los Angeles, Philadelphia, Chicago, Seattle, and even the White House joined in a collective moment of grief and denial that this was reality – that there would be no justice for Michael Brown.[78]

With hindsight affording us a clearer picture of the circumstances leading to Michael Brown's death, we now know that Officer Darren Wilson did not shoot and kill Brown because of the color of his skin. Through the mountain of physical evidence and crime scene data, combined with eyewitness accounts (many of whom retracted their previous statements of Michael Brown's innocence), we now know that Officer Wilson was indeed physically assaulted by Michael Brown. Michael Brown, the prime suspect in a recent robbery, attempted to seize Wilson's weapon from him during that assault. Michael Brown, who was 6'4 and 292lbs, did charge at the officer with malicious intent after the initial scuffle. Wilson was completely justified in making the brutal, split-second decision to take the life of another human being when confronted with the possible loss of his own. Who would have done any differently?

Although the facts of the case proved the initial claims to be demonstrably untrue, to the extent that they cannot be believed by a reasonable person, the narrative that dominated the conversation in Ferguson would eventually force itself into the psyche of a nation – a psyche plugged into social media outlets that, at the time, were developing into the goliaths they have now become. The popular narrative was still that Michael Brown was not killed because he violently assaulted a police officer and attempted to steal that officer's firearm – Michael Brown was killed because the police in America have a disdain for black men. As Patrisse Cullors, co-founder of the Black Lives Matter movement, put it in December of 2014, "We have to shift culture. Darren Wilson killed Mike Brown because he thought he looked like a demon. Policy is not going to shift that. Jim Crow laws are gone, but we still have Jim Crow hate."[79] Slowly but surely, as the national spotlight centered its attention on more police shootings of unarmed black men, Americans were forced to recognize that the way America polices its citizens is irredeemably racist. Or so Critical Thinkers would have us believe.

It's easy to see how a person could fall victim to this depiction of policing in America, and to this Critical Narrative we find ourselves repeating in our heads every time we look to our phones for the latest trending bodycam footage. For the better part of a decade, major news outlets have selectively monetized the tragic deaths of many unarmed black men at the hands of police officers. When one turns on the news or opens Twitter, how could one avoid the torrent of stories flooding one's screens? Critical Thinkers have jumped on this coverage, putting these incidents forward as evidence of their various critical theories. "See, the United States is irredeemably racist!" an activist might say. "Police brutality is a leading cause of death in the black community!"

The Facts

The facts are quite inconvenient for those Critical Thinkers claiming that unarmed black men are being casually murdered in the streets by racist cops. Starting in 2015, in the wake of the death of Michael Brown, the Washington Post began tracking every fatal shooting by an on-duty police officer in the United States. Each year, roughly 1,000 people are killed by the police, a statistic that has remained constant for as long as the Washington Post has been tracking this data. Of these roughly 1,000 people, most of whom are men, an overwhelming majority of incidents involve a violent confrontation between a police officer and a career criminal armed with a gun or a knife.

In 2020, 1,021 people were killed by the police. Of those, 459 were white and 244 were black. As a subset of that data, and more importantly to the radical claim at hand, officers killed 26 unarmed white people and 18 unarmed black people.[80] In both cases, unarmed certainly does not mean the use of lethal force was not wholly justified.

In one such case, 27-year-old Dylan Ray Scott, a white man wanted for grand theft and resisting arrest, was shot and killed by police after trying to flee in his vehicle, which led to a crash.[81] Officers on the scene pleaded with Scott to show his hands, but he refused, insisting that he had a pistol that he was going to use.[82] "I do not want to shoot you, but if you don't show me your hands, that's what is going to happen," a deputy can be heard saying on a bodycam recording of the standoff. Scott turned out to have been unarmed.

In another case that same year, Michael Erich Lewis, a 39-year-old black man with previous convictions of resisting an officer, spousal battery, and failure to register as a sex offender, was shot and killed after reaching into his truck and charging at an officer during a traffic stop. Officers found a firearm at the scene. It was Lewis's gun, but he didn't have it on him when charging at the officer. At that exact moment, he was unarmed.

Year after year and case after case, one finds that nearly all of the unarmed men that meet their end at the hands of police officers are placing those officers in a situation where there is no alternative measure to be taken.

In 2014, just two days after Michael Brown's death, Ezell Ford was shot and killed by LAPD officers. Ford had attacked one of the officers and attempted to remove that officer's firearm from its holster. He had previously been diagnosed with bipolar disorder and schizophrenia. He was technically unarmed as he failed to remove the firearm.

In 2016, Christopher Sowell was shot and killed in Philadelphia after stabbing two boys. After getting into a shootout with deputies after a suspected carjacking, Donnell Thompson was shot and killed in Compton, California. In both cases, the men were unarmed when they were shot.

In 2017, Jean Pedro Pierre was shot and killed in Lauderdale Lakes, Florida, after assaulting a deputy. The assaulted officer had attempted to use a taser and baton to defend himself, but Pierre had been undeterred. A month earlier, Calvin Toney was shot and killed by an officer in Baton Rouge, Louisiana. Toney had tried to take an officer's stun gun and repeatedly refused to back down. In both cases, the men were unarmed.

In many cases, like the ones just described, it would be inconceivable to take the position that these unarmed men did not pose an immediate danger to the lives of our public servants. Are we to suggest that, when confronted with a person attempting to take their firearm, our officers have other measurable actions that they can take to resolve safely the situation in which they find themselves? Are those officers to try and use their taser when a violent felon already has one hand on that officer's firearm? Are those officers to shoot the person assaulting them in the leg? There are only two types of people who can make such suggestions in these scenarios; those who have never been in a serious physical altercation and those who have never used a firearm.

As a subset of the violent and potentially deadly unarmed black and white people killed each year by police officers, you will find an even smaller number of cases that are simply tragic; the only explanation being the evidence of horrific mistakes, bad policing, misconduct or judgment, or sheer and shitty circumstance. George Floyd's death is the one on the tip of everyone's tongue – there never having been a case that catapulted Critical Social Justice activism to the levels we now see. Officer Derek Chauvin knelt on George Floyd for 9 minutes and 29 seconds (not the 8 minutes and 46 seconds that had become "a symbol of police brutality"[83]), during which George Floyd passed away. Floyd posed no serious threat to the officers involved in his death and, even to the untrained eye, he was clearly suffering physical and mental duress. Surely this instance was proof positive that we live in an America that breeds a fundamental disgust for black and brown citizens. The proof of this, Critical Thinkers will say, lies in the fact that these incidents rarely happen to white people. Or do they?

In August 2016, a dispatcher for the Dallas Police Department received a 911 call from a man who suffered from schizophrenia and depression. Thirty-two-year-old Tony Timpa stated he felt afraid and needed help. When they arrived at the scene, officers confronted a man in psychological distress, seemingly unaware of his surroundings and what was happening. Timpa had already been restrained by a local security guard and, visibly confused, struggled and kicked at officers while lying handcuffed in a grassy area as the officers applied back and neck pressure. Timpa pleaded, "Please don't hurt me!" and "Help me!" as officers responded, "We're not going to hurt you. What did you take today?"

"Tony, relax. Tony, relax. Tony, relax. You don't need to be squirming, man. We're trying to get you help," says one of the officers holding the panicked man down. "Let me go, please. Please let me go!" Timpa responded. These calls for help would continue for several minutes as officers determined how best to restrain a man trying to fight his way to his feet. Tony eventually calmed down as officers joked and laughed about what to do next. They asked, "Tony, are you still with us?" and "Is he asleep," after Timpa couldn't sustain his struggle. "Shit, if I was squirming like him, I'd be sleeping too," said one officer. Other jokes followed: "Tony, you're late for school," and "Breakfast, scrambled eggs, your favorite".. Eventually, the comedy would subside as one officer asked, "He ain't dead, is he?" "He didn't just die down there, did he?"[84]

Tony Timpa did die that night after 14 minutes of pressured restraint. The official cause of death was sudden cardiac death due to "the toxic effects of cocaine and the stress associated with physical restraint."[85] For those that have seen both bodycam videos, the similarities between the death of George Floyd and Tony Timpa cannot be ignored. One could make a good argument that the death of Tony Timpa was even more egregious in that the jovial attitude the officers displayed throughout the incident only waned when they realized they had "fucked up."

Tony Timpa's death was a tragic incident of failed policing, much like George Floyd's. In Timpa's case, a federal judge tossed an excessive force lawsuit against the five officers involved in the incident. Four of those officers remain on the force today and Timpa's family received no settlement. His case never rose to national attention. Timpa's death was inconvenient for those espousing Critical Narratives; it didn't fit neatly into the systemic racism accusations so often leveled when a black man dies at the hands of a white police officer, armed or unarmed. Timpa didn't receive the three funeral services that George Floyd received in Texas, Tennessee, and Minnesota, and he wasn't buried in a gold casket. Celebrities didn't rush to demand systemic change. No one changed their profile pictures on social media to signal their unwavering support for justice. Global organizations didn't turn on a dime, committing to "do the work."

Most of us know about the tragic death of 12-year-old Tamir Rice, but we have never heard of 13-year-old Linden Cameron, an unarmed autistic teen who was shot and killed by police in his mother's home while suffering a mental health crisis.[86] We've heard of Trayvon Martin, but not of 17-year-old Hunter Brittain, who was shot by an officer while reaching for an oil can to place behind his truck tire because the vehicle wouldn't shift into park during a traffic stop.[87] We remember Eric Garner, but who can recall the violent beating of mentally ill and homeless man Kelly Thomas by Fullerton Police Department officers in 2011 – a beating so bad that Thomas would never recover from his injuries. He would die just five days after officer Manuel Ramos was recorded saying, "I just smashed his face to hell" on a dashcam recording.[88]

Could it be that Cameron, Brittain, and Thomas didn't receive their due time in the national spotlight because they were not black? You don't hear about the fact that, of the nine people shot and killed by police in Maine in 2017, 8 were white, of which the only unarmed person to die was an 18-year-old white woman.[89] In Texas that same year, of the five unarmed persons shot and killed by the police, three were white, including a 21-year-old woman, and a 6-year-old boy shot twice by stray bullets while playing in his room.[90]

Horrific encounters with police have happened to people of all races, ethnicities, and creeds. It is necessary to demand that those responsible for criminal levels of misconduct that result in the injury or death of our fellow Americans are met by a jury of their peers. However, given the data, it would be intellectually dishonest, if not conspiratorial, to claim that the killing of unarmed black men by police officers in our streets is a systemic problem. Roughly 20 unarmed black men die at the hands of police officers each year, and nearly all of those men are violent criminals who have placed officers in a situation that leaves them no other option than to take a life. Each year police officers kill more unarmed and violent white men for the same reason. In an instance where police kill an unarmed, but violent and possibly deadly black man, the cries for justice ring loud and clear, regardless of whether or not the officer pulling the trigger was justified in doing so. The same cannot be said when an officer guns down a violent and possibly deadly white man for the same reasons. Smart money would bet the house that each time an unarmed man dies at the hands of police, another unarmed man with a different skin color has died under similar circumstances and in nearly the exact same way. Black Americans do not have a monopoly of tragedy involving the police, and the data at hand by no means supports the radical claims proposed by Critical Thinkers.

Violent Crime

When confronted with evidence running contradictory to their claims, Critical Thinkers will often point out that, although more white people are killed each year by police, blacks are still three times as likely to die at the hands of an officer when adjusted for population. Surely this disparity supports the radical claim that America does not value black lives, does it not? If police are killing black men disproportionately, that must imply systemic racism, correct? It is true that blacks are three times more likely to be shot and killed by police in the US than whites, but this statistic is not supportive of the radical claims of Critical Thinkers. No disparity exists in a vacuum. This disparity, like so many others tossed around as proof of radical claims, falls short of its intended landing, only begging us to dive deeper into the disproportionate rates at which a small percentage of Americans commit violent crime.

A white man in Arizona is twice as likely to be imprisoned as a white man in Wisconsin. He is also over 50 percent more likely to be shot and killed by police.[91] What could explain this disparity? It doesn't fit neatly into a Critical Narrative because both groups are white. Are cops in Arizona upholding systems of privilege, power, and oppression that target white people more than Wisconsin cops do? Unlikely. The more reasonable and straightforward answer is that white men in Arizona are committing more violent crimes proportionate to their overall population than the white men in Wisconsin are. In 2017, white men in Arizona committed more than two times the number of murders than their white counterparts in Wisconsin after adjusting for population.[92][93] Is it at all surprising that those who commit violent crimes are locked up more than those who do not? Whites are twice as likely to be locked up in Alabama as they are in Iowa, while at the same time, blacks in Alabama are nearly four times less likely to be imprisoned than blacks in Iowa.[94] Does this mean that Iowa is less likely to imprison violent white criminals? Does it mean that Alabama is less likely to imprison violent black criminals? Of course not. It means that, once one has adjusted for populations, you find that there are more white criminals in Alabama than in Iowa and more black criminals in Iowa than in Alabama.

These types of intraracial disparities exist everywhere, but they are often left out of the Critical Thinkers playbook because they directly refute the idea that the only reason a given disparity can exist is because of "Racism!" The truth is that police officers across the country have a disproportionate number of interactions with criminals because that is precisely what we have tasked them with doing. If we're going to examine why black Americans might be three times as likely to be shot and killed by police, we must examine the disproportionate amount of crime committed by young black men and the consequently disproportionate number of encounters this disparity demands.

In 2017, 643 people were murdered in Chicago, most of whom were black. Most of the men killed were younger than 30, as were most of those pulling the trigger. A whopping 85 percent of all homicides in the city were categorized as either a gang altercation or other dispute and an overwhelming number of the victims and offenders had criminal records. These statistics paint a bleak picture of a city torn apart by gang violence; young black men running around and killing other young black men.

There were over 2,700 shootings in the city that year and nearly 3,500 shooting victims. Most violent clashes happened on a sidewalk or street, leading to regular headlines like this: "Chicago Reels as 3 Children are Gunned Down in 4 Days".[95] Between January and July 2021, there were a reported 172 children shot in the Windy City, of which 25 died. This means that in the first seven months of 2021, a greater number of children died as a result of gang violence in Chicago than the number of unarmed black men who were shot and killed by police in the US in 2017. The youngest victim was a one-month-old who was shot in the head during a "brazen daytime attack near 66th and Halsted Street in Englewood."[96] Street cameras captured the video, and, as you can imagine, it is horrifying. It's hard to arrest those responsible for such acts, given the culture of silence often found in cities plagued by gang violence. When police arrest someone in the city for a crime, there is a 74% chance they are black.[97] The fact is, a small proportion of young black men in Chicago attract a lot of police attention because of the staggering and disproportionate amount of crime they commit.

Although it is not as bad as Chicago, the disproportionate rate at which black Americans commit violent crime is a national trend.

In 2017, 45 percent of those arrested for murder nationally were white (73 percent of the US population is white). That same year, 53 percent of those arrested for murder nationally were black (13 percent of the US population is black).[98] If we focus further on black and white males between the ages of 20-39 – seeing as the infant and elderly black and white populations aren't typically the ones running around committing murder – the statistics are even more staggering. In 2017, white males in that range (11 percent of the U.S. population) were responsible for 17 percent of the nation's murders, and black males in that range (2 percent of the U.S. population) were responsible for 23 percent.[99] This means that, for both blacks and whites, a small and incredibly violent portion of the population is doing most of the murdering. If we are trying to understand how blacks might be three times as likely to be killed by an officer, we cannot ignore that the fact young black men are egregiously overrepresented in precisely the types of scenarios you would hope to find police involved in. If you are a violent criminal, it is only a matter of time before you find yourself near an officer charged with the task of removing you from the street. According to the Bureau of Justice Statistics, black Americans murder at seven times the rate of white Americans. Are we to pretend that this disparity will produce an equal proportion of encounters between blacks and whites with police?

Critical Thinkers would have us all believe that black men are casually murdered by racist police officers every day in America. The numbers just don't add up. Police rarely kill unarmed black men, and when they do there is an overwhelming chance that the "unarmed" categorization is significantly misleading at best or a purposeful deception at worst. Police shoot unarmed white men in the same circumstances and in larger numbers. Although blacks are more likely to be shot and killed by police, it's because black men commit a disproportionate number of violent crimes which demand officer attention. When the Washington Post runs articles with headlines like, "Police killing black people is a pandemic, too," they spread a

Critical Narrative of policing that is so demonstrably untrue that it should be considered journalistic malpractice.[100] Yet, the incessant hammering continues. An officer can't even shoot a person who is actively attempting murder – as was the case with Ma'Khia Bryant – without the president of the United States alluding to "systemic racism" as the culprit.

If these facts aren't enough to convince Critical Thinkers that we don't have a systemically racist policing agenda in the United States, consider this – the crime rates for black Americans drop precipitously as we widen our gaze to include all of those terrible fascists and racists we know are hiding out in "the country." Nearly 40 percent of black Americans live in the suburbs, and 25 percent live in either small metropolitan areas or rural communities.[101] If we examine the percent distribution of arrests for various categories of crime for non-metropolitan areas by race in 2017, we discover that blacks are underrepresented in arrests for total arrests, burglary, larceny-theft, motor vehicle theft, arson, vandalism, driving under the influence, liquor laws, drunkenness, and curfew and loitering law violations. The percentage distribution for black boys under 18 arrested for drug abuse violation is 10.3 percent, less than half that of the rate for metropolitan counties.[102] We don't have a systemic policing problem in this country – we have a systemic inner-city crime catastrophe that has been inadequately addressed because moral busybodies are rampaging through college campuses, boardrooms, and the halls of Congress with their Critical Thinking caps on, utterly incapable of addressing the real issues faced by our country's most disenfranchised populations.

It is miraculous that we don't see more cases like George Floyd and Tony Timpa each year. Over 800,000 officers in this country are involved in hundreds of millions of police-public interactions. In 2017, more than 10 million of those interactions involved an arrest.[103] Given these astounding numbers and the innumerable complexities and incoherent randomness of any given situation, is it reasonable to expect that we will ever have a year without cases like that of

Tamir Rice and Kameron Prescott? There isn't a reasonable person in the world who would disagree that there are some terrible police officers, just like there are terrible doctors, lawyers, and businessmen. Police carry firearms and are tasked with placing themselves into the most dangerous situations that any member of our society can place themselves in. What number of bad officers is tolerable before the whole system must be dismantled? If a Critical Thinker's answer is "zero," by what means can that be achieved?

CHAPTER FIVE

POLICING DISMANTLED

> "Ideology – that is what gives evildoing its long-sought justification and gives the evildoer the necessary steadfastness and determination."
>
> –Aleksandr Solzhenitsyn,
> *The Gulag Archipelago*

Covid-19 pandemic anxiety was at an all-time high. Millions were unemployed. Legacy media organizations were feeding Americans a radical claim that black men were being regularly slaughtered by cops. And then there was George Floyd.

According to the Insurance Information Institute, May 26th – June 8th, 2020 was the "costliest civil disorder in U.S. history," surpassing the LA riots that followed from the acquittal of Los Angeles Police Officers after their vicious beating of Rodney King. The Property Claim Services unit designated these 14 days as a "multi-state catastrophe event."[104]

There were nearly 8,000 demonstrations linked to the Black Lives Matter movement across more than 2,000 locations in all 50 states and Washington, DC. Although the majority were peaceful, hundreds of these protests erupted into widespread looting and rioting. These riots would come with an estimated $2 billion price tag.

Minneapolis received the worst of it with a nearly five-mile stretch of unmitigated destruction. The 3rd Precinct was abandoned before being burned to the ground. The New York Times reported that "Fires and looting destroyed hundreds of businesses, among them a worker-owned bicycle co-op, a historic diner run by a husband and wife, and the new headquarters of a nonprofit organization that works with Native American teens." In all, 267 restaurants, 207 retail outlets, 114 service businesses, 85 grocery stores, 76 cellphone stores, 63 gas stations, 60 auto workshops, 53 residences, 52 salons, and 47 healthcare businesses in Minneapolis and St. Paul suffered anything from broken windows and looting to complete annihilation.

After years of Critical Thinkers forcing radical claims into the mainstream, buttressed by legacy media institutions monetizing every conceivable bodycam recording, America had developed the critical consciousness of Herbert Marcuse's dreams. One Yale professor described this moment in history as a "great opportunity" to "challenge the nation's prevailing psychology."[105]

Major corporations took to social media to pledge solidarity with the Black Lives Matter popular movement. On Instagram, Netflix posted, "To be silent is to be complicit. Black lives matter." Apple echoed the sentiment, posting of their determination "to speak and act against racism and injustice of all kinds."

Hollywood used heavyweight celebrities to let the world know it was time to stand against racism. In partnership with the NAACP, Hollywood's white elite released a video titled "Take responsibility." In it, Julianne Moore declared that black Americans were being "slaughtered in the streets." Sarah Paulson, famous for her roles in *American Horror Story*, equated being black with a death sentence.

Dozens of collegiate and professional sporting organizations rushed to put out their solidarity statements. Mike Krzyzewski, five-time national champion coach of Duke's Men's Basketball team, released a video statement saying, "Do we not see the problem, the disease, the plague that has been with our country for four centuries? Do we not see systemic racism and social injustice? Come on!"[106]

The message was clear. It is no longer acceptable to call the fight for social justice a political topic. It was no longer acceptable to ask questions, disagree, or remain silent. It is not enough to critique the world against the Critical Thinker's vision – one must instead actively seek to dismantle it.

Defund the Police

Critical Thinkers, many of whom held positions of power as Congressmen, Mayors, and City Council Members, used America's racial anxiety to usher in radical agendas and begin dismantling police departments nationwide. "Defund the police" became their rallying cry.

In Minneapolis, the epicenter of America's racial reckoning, a veto-proof majority of the City Council approved a proposal to eliminate the city's police department. Speaking of the reform, Minneapolis city council president Lisa Bender said that, "Our efforts at incremental reform have failed, period. Our commitment is to do what's necessary to keep every single member of our community safe and to tell the truth: that the Minneapolis police are not doing that. Our commitment is to end policing as we know it and to recreate systems of public safety that actually keep us safe."[107]

The proposal submitted by the Minneapolis City council called for the creation of a Department of Community Safety and Violence Prevention. This new body would have "responsibility for public safety services prioritizing a holistic, public health-oriented approach."[108] As part of this new approach, "licensed peace officers" and "restorative justice" practices would be used in lieu of traditional policing.

In Austin, Texas, City Council members cut the police department budget by $150 million. They reinvested the funds into mental health response units, violence prevention, housing, and substance abuse programs.[109] Roughly $50 million was allocated toward a "Reimagine Safety Fund." With these dollars, the City Manager and City Council would invest in radical goals like ending the racial disparities in policing. By the year 2023, the Austin Police Department would be held accountable for achieving "zero racial disparities in traffic stops and citations," "zero use of force incidents," and "zero deaths at the hands of Austin Police Department (APD) officers."[110]

Mayor London Breed of San Francisco also cut police funding. In July 2020, she announced that $120 million would be redirected from policing to the community. In a video statement, Breed said that "We are listening to the community and prioritizing investments into the African American community around housing, mental health and wellness, workforce development, economic justice, education, advocacy, and accountability."[111]

Dozens of other major cities voted to defund their police department in 2020, including New York, Chicago, Seattle, Milwaukee, Philadelphia, and Baltimore.[112] But this was only a disruption, a way for Critical Thinkers to get in the door. The goal is to dismantle policing entirely.

Critical Criminology

The "defund the police" movement is only a single maneuver in a much broader war to dismantle policing as we know it in the United States – a scheme designed to destabilize America's conception of crime and justice. The Critical Thinker's goal is not to simply rearrange funds from police departments to some reimagined form of public safety. It is to create a society in which crime is no longer considered criminal.

Critical Criminology is a critical theory of crime. Critical Criminologists argue that crime is the product of power and oppression. Like Karl Marx, Critical Criminologists argue that capitalist systems inevitably produce conflict and crime due to a systemic power imbalance between those who own property and those who do not.

Borrowing from the neo-Marxist tradition, Critical Criminologists argue that this imbalance of power is not just an economic one – it also passes through racial, gendered, and ethnic lines. The Critical Criminologist's job is to critique systems of crime and policing against a moral vision of what those things should look like. Like all moral visions of Critical Thinkers, this vision is one in which all peoples are equally represented in crime and punishment data. Any disparity between large groups is an indication that the Critical Criminologist has found a site of oppression that must be dismantled.

Critical Criminologists claim that powerful hegemonic forces (Gramsci, anyone?) shape our political discussions and practices of crime and policing. The Critical Criminologist's job is to reveal these forces for what they are argued to be – forms of control – and then build "counter-hegemonic coalitions" to begin the dismantling process.

Critical Thinkers see the American policing system not as an entity to protect the victims of crime, ensure public safety, and secure liberty and property for all, but as a mechanism to enforce an inherently unjust capitalistic and liberal society that produces unequal outcomes between groups. They see it as a means of keeping those without power on the bottom of the totem pole, and a way of keeping subordinate groups marginalized and in check. Critical Thinkers see the police as nothing more than bourgeoisie strongmen enforcing institutionalized inequality.

"There are diverse Marxist perspectives in criminology, but, in general, compared with the labelling theorists and the conflict theorists, Marxist criminologists espouse more radical views about the origins of crime and deviance. This means that they trace the origins of crime and deviance, and, indeed, other social problems, such as class and racial inequality, to what they consider to be an unequal and unjust social and economic order that must be dismantled." (Ugwudike, *An Introduction to Critical Criminology*.)

Critical Thinkers believe that American cops only serve to protect and secure the "unjust social and economic order" of the group at the top of the social and economic hierarchy – straight white men. In their view, liberalism and capitalism are evil and dominant groups use the police to protect this framework, and thus to secure and protect their power and privilege.

What can be considered an everyday street crime is not to be viewed as an individual act of deviance committed by a rational actor. We are to regard it as the inevitable result of capitalism and liberalism. In the most extreme interpretations, those who commit crimes are justified in breaking the law. Theft of private property, for instance, isn't considered a problem because the very fact that some are allowed to have private property is the cause of injustice. In the Critical Thinker's view, when police are called to secure private property, what they are really doing is protecting the very thing that gives an unequal distribution of wealth and power to some while preventing others from accessing their fair share. Some Critical Thinkers argue that those who benefit from the hegemonic control of dominant groups didn't earn their property. Therefore, they have no inherent right to have it.

Critical Thinkers have taken up Critical Criminology to demand widespread and systemic change of not only our police departments but our economy, politics, and educational systems. Knowing this can help one understand how the conversation moved on from condemning individual police officers to advocating for "economic justice" as mayor London Breed of San Francisco has.

Critical Thinkers maintain that criminal behavior is simply an "expression of resistance by the subservient classes against exploitative social relations."[113] They don't want to police those acts of resistance; they want to encourage them. And that's precisely what they are doing.

Redefining Crime

In our post-George Floyd world, Critical Thinkers have quintupled down on their radical claim that unequal outcomes between groups are in and of themselves evidence of systemic discrimination. To break the system which sees black men overrepresented in criminal data, Critical Thinkers are reforming laws and redefining crime. They consider it racist to believe that human beings are individual agents capable of deciding whether or not to commit a crime. Critical Thinkers deem criminal law itself a means of controlling marginalized groups by enforcing unequal social and economic outcomes.

California has become incredibly lax with crimes that would see more black Americans represented in the state's crime data. Black Americans commit an over representative share of shoplifting thefts in The Golden State. Rather than trying to deter more shoplifting, which would undoubtedly be considered racist over-policing, Californians took to the polls in 2014 to vote "yes" to Proposition 47. This Proposition passed and recategorized property theft of $950 or less from a felony to a misdemeanor.

With police resources stretched to their limits after Mayor London Breed's $120 million budget cut in 2020, shop owners were left to fend for themselves while being actively robbed in broad daylight. One need only to search for "San Francisco shoplifting" on your favorite internet browser to see how disastrously this policy has played out. In most videos, would-be shoplifters casually walk into stores and openly fill their bags with whichever products they need, careful not to exceed the $950 stipend given to them. In others, large groups take their time clearing out entire store shelves.

Misdemeanor crimes are much less likely to be investigated, let alone prosecuted. Store owners and security personal are for their part less likely to do anything to stop brazen criminals for fear of being labeled a racist (if the perpetrator is black or brown) or getting hurt. It is widely understood that Walgreens and CVS stores have open-door policies for those wishing to acquire a five-finger discount.

In Chicago, the situation is even more ridiculous. Criminals have a new, sure-fire way to avoid being arrested by the Chicago Police Department (CPD) – they run.

On May 26th, 2021, Mayor Lori Lightfoot and CPD Superintendent David O. Brown announced a new foot pursuit policy as a larger effort to "transform the police department through reform."[114] As part of this new policy, officers will need to "ask themselves if the need to apprehend the subject is worth the risk to the responding officers, the public, or the subject." Additionally, officers are not to pursue a suspect if they feel they couldn't control that suspect in a confrontation.

As defined, there aren't many situations in which an officer could justify chasing a suspected criminal, especially when one considers the consequences. The new policy proposes that officers face disciplinary charges if they are found to be in violation of it. It also explicitly bans any disciplinary action taken against the officer for choosing not to engage in a foot pursuit. In what world would an officer put his career on the line under such regulation? In what world would a criminal not be incentivized to get out of Dodge?

Baltimore, America's violent crime capital, has stopped prosecuting drug possession, attempted distribution, prostitution, trespassing, minor traffic offenses, and urinating or defecating in public. In a press release, the State's Attorney and Mayor's Office hailed this decision as a "progressive direction" that would "address the systemic inequity of mass incarceration."[115]

In Philadelphia, officers can no longer investigate and stop people from urinating in public, gambling, carrying open liquor bottles, or loitering. These quality-of-life offenses are said to contribute to racial policing disparities and, as long as the offender stops doing what they are doing when asked, the city will press no charges.[116]

The idea that the United States should radically redefine crime to artificially engineer criminal diversity data is insane. The argument that unjust laws target black American men and force them into a prison pipeline for committing petty crimes is simply not borne out by the data.

According to the latest data from the Bureau of Justice Statistics, there were 1.2 million sentenced prisoners under the jurisdiction of state correctional authorities in 2018. Of these, 394,800 were white and 409,600 were black. For Critical Thinkers, the argument stops here. There is nothing to be gleaned from this information other than the fact that black Americans are vastly overrepresented in the state prison system. To a Critical Thinker, this must imply unjust criminal codes and police conduct.

But when one digs deeper, a different picture emerges. Nearly 62 percent of black Americans in state correctional facilities are there for violent crimes, including 17.3 percent for murder, 19.1 percent for robbery, and 12.3 percent for aggravated assault. Only 12.7 percent of the black correctional population is confined because of drug charges, including only 3 percent for possession. Those numbers are 16.3 percent and 5.1 percent, respectively, for the white state correctional population.

Black American men are not being targeted and sent to prison for petty street crimes. They are overwhelmingly sent to prison for violent crimes. The same can be said for Hispanic Americans (61.6 percent) and, to a lesser extent, (48.3 percent) white Americans. Violent crimes have victims, and it is the criminal justice system's job to protect law-abiding citizens from having their liberty and property seized by those who would do them harm.

But Critical Thinkers do not care about these facts. They are trained to critique and dismantle everything. They fundamentally believe that all human life can be boiled down to power dynamics expressed along the lines of class, race, gender, and ethnicity. When given positions of power, Critical Thinkers act on this impulse. In this case, they force everyone else to buy into their conspiracy, demanding society change its perception of justice. In their view, it's not the criminal who is to blame – it is the system. The system is forcing people to commit crimes. Therefore, while dismantling capitalism and liberalism is the ultimate goal, they will settle for the incremental step of defunding the police and decriminalizing certain crimes to destabilize society and force equal outcomes.

For the poorest members of our society, acting on this delusion has dire consequences.

Consequences: From Floyd to Now

At the height of the George Floyd riots, CNN anchor Chris Cuomo took to the air to explain his thoughts on the violence unfolding before the nation. Under a breaking news chyron that read, "NYC BRACING FOR UNREST AFTER NIGHT OF WIDESPREAD LOOTING; CURFEW BEGAN AT 8PM ET" he stated:

"Now, too many see the protests as the problem. No, the problem is what forced your fellow citizens to take to the streets: persistent and poisonous inequities and injustice. And please, show me where it says protestors are supposed to be polite and peaceful."[117]

Others shared similar sentiments. Colin Kaepernick took to Twitter to write, "When civility leads to death, revolting is the only logical reaction. The cries for peace will rain down, and when they do, they will land on deaf ears, because your violence has brought this resistance."

Millions of Americans watched as looters and rioters set cities ablaze in the weeks following the death of George Floyd. The actions of those burning buildings and robbing liquor stores were often said to be justified. "It's just property," one family member told me. "They have insurance."

But it wasn't "just property." The buildings burned and looted represented years of sweat and toil. Most businesses fail and, if someone happens to make it out alive, the investment comes at astronomical costs. Business owners spend years, if not decades, risking everything on a single goal to try and build a better future for their families. Insurance can't replace that investment. Forcing someone to start from scratch after a lifetime of struggle is cruel and immoral. And it wasn't just "white people's" property that was lost.

For seven years, Chris Montana fought tooth and nail to make his first business successful. His distillery, Du Nord, was a popular spot in Minneapolis. That is, until rioters ransacked the place. In an interview with NPR, Montana said:

"They set multiple fires. They stole our inventory. I found cases of our booze all up and down the street. And it was the sprinkler system coming on and putting about a foot of water in the entire warehouse: that's what did most of the damage. It feels like someone punched you in the face."[118]

College student and entrepreneur Elliott Broaster had only been in business for two years when looters ransacked his business on May 31, 2020. Smoke n' Things wasn't just a business; it was an "incubator for a lot of kids of color." Broaster described it as a spot where young would-be business owners learned how to use Shopify, sign a lease, and fund merchandise.

Rioters smashed Broaster's storefront windows and merchandise, stole most of his product, and even pissed on the floor. When interviewed, Broaster stated that "I put so much time, energy, and headaches into this business. For someone to destroy it in a matter of seconds – that really hurts. It's about more than just capital; it's emotional trauma."[119]

Chris Montana and Elliott Broaster are just two of the 2.6 million black business owners in the United States. Most of these businesses are sole proprietorships, representing an individual American's absolute risk and total investment into their dream. But none of that matters to a Critical Thinker. Law and order, crime and policing must all be dismantled. Nothing will stop the march of Critical Social Justice, not even destroying the lives of those one is said to be fighting for.

And businesses weren't the only collateral damage in May, June, and July of 2020.

At 77-years-old, retired St. Louis Police captain David Dorn rushed to the defense of a friend's pawn shop during the early hours of June 2nd.[120] He was shot and killed, left on the sidewalk to take his last breath after serving his community for 38 years. He was black.

On May 29, 2020, 53-year-old security officer David Patrick Underwood was shot and killed while guarding the Ronald V. Dellums Federal Building in Oakland, CA. He was black.

On the night of May 30, former Indiana University football player Chris Beaty was shot and killed. Beaty's last text message read, "I'm bout to walk around my block now to make sure my building is good." He was black.[121]

This level of lawlessness and violence destabilizes communities. It's hard to go to work when rioters have burned down your employer's business. It's hard to shop for groceries and maintain your vehicle when there is no longer a grocery store or auto repair shop in your community. The "it's just property" crowd may get off on the thought of a Target or Walgreens burning down – those things represent the evils of capitalism. But that crowd doesn't have to live there. They don't have to wake up every day and wonder where you might go to get essential goods and services; wonder where your next paycheck is coming from; wonder if your neighborhood hasn't yet seen just how bad things can get when the cops are defunded, hamstrung, and stretched to breaking point.

Many of the George Floyd looters and rioters were not Critical Thinkers. They were bad actors taking advantage of a terrible situation which had been exacerbated by Critical Thinkers forcing radical claims into the national race discourse for decades. But it didn't matter that many of them weren't Critical Thinkers. What mattered was that Critical Thinkers had successfully manufactured a crisis that would usher in the proper dismantling process.

Minnesota saw significant upticks in violent crime in 2020. Murders rose 58.1 percent, robberies 26.1 percent, and aggravated assault 21.7 percent. In Minneapolis, more than 200 police officers quit or went on extended leave after the death of George Floyd. Cops were fed up with being told they were vile racists, sick of threats to defund and dismantle their departments, tired of the lack of support and constant demonization. These officers were done living with the fear that they or their families would be targeted with violence for simply doing their jobs.

What little remains of the Minneapolis Police Force changed the way it policed communities in 2020. From June 1, 2020 – May 31, 2021, there was a 74 percent reduction in traffic stops, a 76 percent reduction in patrolling known problem areas, and a 69 percent reduction in walking foot beats.[122] With such a drawback, Minneapolis has descended into chaos – chaos described by one black resident as a "gangster's paradise."[123]

In North Minneapolis, five children – all under the age of 10 – were shot during a two-month span in 2021. Speaking after a three-year-old child was shot while playing outside, Bishop Harding Smith, a community church leader, said that, "We are losing a generation of our young people. Lawlessness has taken over. These murders are crippling our community and it's devastating our neighborhood."[124] At the time of writing, not one of those responsible for these shootings is in jail.

Like the death of George Floyd, the demonization and defunding of police echoed across the nation. In 2020, the United States experienced the most significant murder spike ever recorded – nearly 30 percent.[125] It is reasonable to conclude that the covid-19 pandemic played a part here. Still, given the situation in places like

Minneapolis, it is entirely unreasonable to conclude that the covid-19 pandemic was the primary driver of such dramatic change.

For instance, the homicide rate in Denver, CO, jumped 50 percent in 2020. A group of researchers studied the causes of such a dramatic increase, concluding that all available data pointed to a legitimacy crisis in American policing.

The researchers contrasted data from before the covid-19 pandemic, and before and after the death of George Floyd, finding that the increase in violent crime before Floyd's death was "indistinguishable" from the violent crime before Covid-19. In other words, violent crime didn't rise due to the covid-19 pandemic; it took off after George Floyd died.

The researchers studying the Denver policing data cited officers pulling back after unrelenting public scrutiny, as they had in Minneapolis, to be a significant factor in the violent crime wave. They added that "depleted trust in the law means citizens will think twice about calling the police to report crimes or suspicious behaviors" and that "delegitimacy of the law emboldens criminal offending populations, as the moral obligation to follow the law is weakened."[126] These factors resulted in nearly 1,000 fewer police stops each week, a "remarkable reduction in police activity."

With less police-public interaction, more illegal guns are left in the hands of violent offenders that should be incarcerated. And poor neighborhoods often bear the consequences. The researchers studying the rise in violent crime in Denver concluded their report with the following statement;

"Neighborhoods that have endured high rates of violence bore the brunt of these trends, often Denver's Black and Latino communities. For example, after Floyd's death, police stops declined by 62% in Northeast Park Hill while violent crime rose by 69%, while East Colfax saw stops fall by 59%, only for violence to jump by 28%. Residents of communities that suffer from violence regularly say that they don't want less policing, but better policing."[127]

Critical Policing

The "defund the police" movement was a single maneuver in the Critical Thinker's battle plan to dismantle policing in the United States. And it wasn't as successful as Critical Thinkers hoped it would be. As violent crime spiked in 2020 and 2021, Americans called on their elected officials, demanding that they do more to keep communities safe. Many of these calls came from those poor, inner-city communities most brutalized by violence.

In Minneapolis, where the city council voted to entirely dismantle the police department in June of 2020, $8 million was diverted from law enforcement to other city services. Since then, however, an additional $6 million has been allocated to hire more police officers.[128]

In New York, Mayor Bill De Blasio initially promised to strip $1 billion from the city's law enforcement budget. In the end, however, less than half of that money would be cut, and only for the 2021 budget.[129]

But the defund the police movement isn't really about defunding the police. It's not about bringing more accountability to police forces or calling for more fiscal responsibility. It's about reimagining public safety, which means reengineering society to align with the Critical Thinker's conception of justice.

The Critical Thinker believes that criminals are victims who cannot be blamed for committing crimes. Societal forces have imposed their will upon him, forcing his hand. Unequal distribution of power and privilege is the root cause. Policing is the act by which those at the top of the power and privilege hierarchy enforce their will upon the marginalized.

If you are attempting to dismantle this system, you cannot stop at defunding police departments. Removing police funding may limit the number of police officers on the street, but it will not fundamentally alter how liberal society conceives of the crimes those officers are charged to enforce. For the Critical Thinker, crime itself must be decriminalized. Stealing $950 of goods from Walgreens isn't a crime in their view; it is the "expression of resistance by the subservient classes against exploitative social relations." A community riddled with prostitution, drug markets, and open defecation isn't full of people trouncing on the liberties of others; it is full of oppressed peoples in open resistance.

Justice can broadly be defined as a principle of fairness. Justice is what happens when we use neutral laws to judge someone fairly and determine whether or not we must punish them for breaking a societal contract. In a just society, the victim of a crime is sacred. Something was stolen from them – their liberty, property, or life – and it is up to society to determine how they are to be repaid for the injustice done to them. It is also up to society to decide what to do with the guilty party, manage criminal behavior, and punish those who cause harm to others.

Critical Thinkers are seeking to dismantle justice. In their view, society is not and has never been just. This is why they are constantly reframing the policing discourse in the United States into one where the criminal is considered the victim. It is why they are OK with cities burning, redefining crime and criminal conduct to allow more of it, and why they are utterly apathetic about the consequences of their actions.

What does it mean when Critical Thinkers demand that police departments produce zero racial disparities in arrests and imprisonment? What does it mean when people who deal drugs and openly shit in public are no longer prosecuted for doing so? In 2021, the crime wave in Los Angeles was so bad that the head of the Police union, Jamie McBride, told tourists to stay out of the city.

"We can't guarantee your safety. It is really, really out of control. I said it to people before, it's like that movie *Purge*, you know, instead of 24 hours to commit your crime, these people have 365 days to commit whatever they want."[130] Just because the Critical Thinker redefines crime, and how we police it, does not mean it no longer exists.

Young, inner-city black men commit a disproportionate share of violent crime. Simply deciding not to police violent offenders any longer to artificially deflate some numbers doesn't change the fact that too many young black men are devastating themselves and their communities. The most antiracist thing one can do is protect the vulnerable, law-abiding, red-white-and-blue blooded Americans from the dictates of those that would rob them of their liberties. Critical Thinkers should do well to think more critically about that.

CHAPTER SIX

EDUCATION

> "Human beings are born with different capacities. If they are free, they are not equal. And if they are equal, they are not free."
>
> –Aleksandr Solzhenitsyn, *The Gulag Archipelago*

There is a wave of reform washing over America's educational system. Critical Thinkers are rushing to disrupt and dismantle color-blind and meritocratic educational frameworks in favor of race-conscious instruction and subjective standards. No longer are all children expected to reach for excellence under an umbrella of neutral principles. Instead, they must be treated on the basis of "from each according to their ability, to each according to their needs".

In the San Diego Unified School District, students are no longer held accountable for turning their homework in on time. Teachers no longer factor classroom misbehavior into a student's grades. In Madison, WI, educators have implemented a new "grading floor" of

40 percent. No student can score lower on a test or assignment.[131] In Oregon, students can now graduate from high school without demonstrating basic math, reading, and writing proficiency.[132]

This attempt to reduce high academic expectations and rigorous standards is calculated. Too many black and brown children fail to achieve at the same levels as their white and Asian peers. To account for this gap in achievement, educators and administrators are attempting to change the rules of the game. In their view, nothing can explain this gap but systemic racism. It has wholly corrupted American education, on the basis that, only through radical political movements within schools can the mechanisms of this system be discovered, uprooted, and dismantled.

For decades, researchers in the United States have studied the differences between high- and low-achieving students of all socioeconomic and demographic backgrounds. Their findings universally suggest that poverty plays the preeminent role in the formation of achievement gaps. That is to say, researchers find that high-achieving children are generally not living in poverty, whereas lower-achieving children typically are. Racism is very real, but it is not the cause of the systemic underachievement of black and brown children.

Until recently, Americans have accepted the evidence put forward by researchers attempting to explain achievement gaps between children. That is, they did until Critical Thinkers assumed enough cultural and political control to see to it that their interpretation bludgeoned its way into the national psyche.

In 2003, most Americans thought the achievement gap was largely explained by three factors; parental involvement, home life and upbringing, and interest on the part of the students.[133] In other words, a majority of Americans agreed with the conclusions drawn by researchers. Americans understood that a student's achievement was significantly impacted by whether or not that student was born into a home with married and involved parents.

But things have changed. In 2021, simply implying that the achievement gaps we see between groups of children have anything to do with marriage rates or parental involvement is immediately to invite accusations of racism. Critical Thinkers have convinced educators and administrators that things like standardized tests are the real driver of unequal achievement. Writing for Black Perspectives in 2016, Ibram X. Kendi said that "Standardized tests have become the most effective racist weapon ever devised to objectively degrade Black minds and legally exclude their bodies."[134] That's right – color-blind and objective assessments of one's reading and math ability should now be considered a tool of white supremacy.

Traditional or radical explanations aside, the achievement gap between black and white children in the United States is very real. In 2019, the average 4th-grade black student in the U.S. scored 25 points below the average 4th-grade white student on the math portion of the National Assessment of Educational Progress (NAEP). Black students also scored lower on the 4th-grade reading assessment and the 8th-grade math and reading assessments. Year after year, black students have lower median SAT scores and are less likely to graduate from high school when compared to white students.

Schools in San Diego, Madison, and Oregon, operating under the assumption that systemic racism is causing the achievement gap, are lowering their academic standards. This is a radical, political move to practice Critical Theory in the classroom. It's an attempt to force equal outcomes out of their students. The Critical Thinkers in these systems ignore decades of research that concludes that poverty – not race – is the driving factor of student achievement.

The Achievement Gap: Early Childhood

The two most significant predictors of a child's academic achievement are parental education and family income. The achievement gap between the 90th percentile of the family income distribution and the 10th percentile is nearly double that of the black and white achievement gap.[135] This means that by the 8th grade, students in the 10th percentile of the family income distribution are almost four years behind those in the 90th percentile.

We first notice these achievement gaps when children are very young, well before they enter school. Poor children as young as two have lower cognitive function than their less poor peers. By the time these children are four, they are often testing six months behind those children of higher-income parents in reading and seven months behind children of higher-income parents in math. Understanding how these early childhood gaps manifest themselves can clarify the persistent gaps between poor and non-poor children observed in later years. As Jane Waldfogel and Elizabeth Washbrook point out in the book *Persistence, Privilege, and Parenting*, the "inequality in school readiness is an important contributor to inequality of later achievement, as evidence shows that half or more of gaps in educational outcomes are already present at school entry."[136]

The achievement gaps between poor and non-poor children begin with the achievement gaps between mothers. Whether a mother is poor or not is strongly correlated with her achievement and whether or not she is married before having children. According to research conducted by the Brookings Institute, Americans have a roughly 2 percent chance of living in poverty if they follow these three steps: finish high school, get a full-time job, and wait until age 21 to get married and have children.[137] Most children living in poverty today are living with a parent or parents that either did not complete high school, does not work full-time, or had children outside of wedlock. In the most impoverished children, we find mothers and fathers who, for one reason or many, misstepped during all three of these critical adulthood junctures.

A college education is an excellent indicator that a woman has followed the crucial steps outlined above. College-educated women are more likely to be married and less likely to have children before marriage. Only 10 percent of women with bachelor's degrees have children outside of wedlock, compared to 59 percent of those with only a high school diploma or GED.[138] Having two married parents significantly decreases one's chances of living in poverty. Having two college-educated parents nearly erases poverty altogether. Poverty, marriage, and education are all strongly correlated. Some children are born to married and college-educated mothers. Many are not.

Children born to married parents perform better on early literacy and numeracy assessments than children born to a single mother.[139] This is probably because children born to married parents have more social and material resources to draw from. They generally aren't worried about where the next meal is coming from or whether or not they'll make new friends when moving to yet another apartment complex. Their quality of food is generally better and their neighborhood safer. Mom and Dad can divvy up household chores, so there is always someone from whom to receive attention. They have twice the kin resources to help ensure their environment is stable, and they have plenty of birthday presents and Christmas cards to look forward to. They are less likely to experience childhood trauma and behavioral problems and more likely to have access to excellent healthcare. In short, the children born to married parents generally have less stress and more support than those born to single parents.

But poverty not only affects what social and material resources a child can draw from – it also affects how a child is parented. In her book *Unequal Childhoods*, Annette Lareau explains that middle-class parents "tend to adopt a cultural logic of child-rearing that stresses the concerted cultivation of children."[140] This "concerted cultivation" means that middle-class parents "deliberately try to stimulate their children's development and foster their cognitive and social skills." Middle-class parents fill their child's leisure time with activities and learning that are meant to result in some desired outcome. Namely, they want to help orient their children in the world to maximize that child's future success. This means their child must know how to read, write, and problem-solve at an early age. They must understand how to interact with others and learn what social displays are permissible.

Middle-class parents often rose to middle-class status by means of their own education (whether that be college or learning a trade). From a very early age, they cultivate their infant children to achieve that same end.

"For working-class and poor families," writes Lareau, "sustaining children's natural growth is viewed as an accomplishment." These families stop short of concerted cultivation, in part because they focus entirely on providing their children with the basics – food, shelter, and healthcare. Single moms and dads have a distinct disadvantage when compared to married parents. They aren't able to rely on another person to share in the responsibility of raising a child. They must primarily manage everything on their own. Even if they are married, working-class or poor parents tend to be less educated. They have less personal experience to draw on when thinking about how best to prepare their child for a rapidly changing workforce. For example, they may not know just how important math achievement will be if their child wants to one day work in the ever-lucrative STEM fields. If they know the importance, they may have only a 5th-grade proficiency in math – not exactly the mastery needed to be comfortable helping your child with their homework.

The concerted cultivation of children can have enormous payoffs. For instance, college-educated mothers read and speak more to their children. This additional stress results in a significant "word gap" between families along socioeconomic lines. One study, published in the American Journal of Speech-Language Pathology, found that "Children whose mothers graduated from college were exposed to 3,000 or so more words per day, translating into a four-million-word gap by four years of age between the highest and lowest SES groups."[141] That gap jumps to nearly 30 million words when comparing only the top and bottom 2 percent of families.

College-educated mothers not only speak and read to their children more often – they are more intentional when doing so. Rather than saying, "Good job!" when a child rolls a ball along the kitchen floor, a college-educated mother might say, "Good job! You rolled the ball across the floor." The child not only hears more words, but they also hear how those words are associated with other words and into which contexts those words are used. Adding up a few dozen or so instances of this intentional focus on language exploration with a child each day can profoundly affect that child's vocabulary and the pace at which they learn. The faster that children can understand how language interfaces with the world around them, the faster they can absorb that world and understand how it works.

Educated mothers also have access to more robust vocabularies than those with less education. It's hard to help foster the development of a large vocabulary in one's toddler if your vocabulary is limited. You may simply not have the words. Generally, mothers with college educations have the most robust vocabularies. But mothers with high school diplomas also have more robust vocabularies than those without them. Rural mothers in Ecuador are nearly universally poor but, all else being equal, some children are born to more educated mothers. As one researcher explains, "Even in settings where poverty is widespread, as is the case in rural Ecuador, children of mothers with lower education and lower vocabulary levels have worse cognitive outcomes than other children do before they enter school."[142] Again, the achievement gaps we see between children start with Mom. Child poverty can correlate with many things, but it most often represents mothers' and fathers' decisions and the achievement gaps between parents. These decisions and achievement gaps influence the development of young children in significant ways.

The Achievement Gap: School

The achievement gaps between groups of children do not seem to narrow once a child starts school. If anything, they tend to grow as disparate socioeconomic groups of children progress through the K-12 system. Critical Thinkers often attribute the growing achievement disparity between poor and non-poor children to the fact that non-poor children attend better-funded schools than do poor children. Although it is true that wealthier families tend to live in areas that can generate more tax revenue for their schools, it is not true that poor and non-poor children always attend schools with significant funding disparities.

Americans underestimate how much the nation is spending per student on schooling each year. Some 55 percent of Americans believe we spend $5,000 or less per student when the actual figure is nearly $11,500.[143] When one studies the amount of State and Federal dollars poured into school districts, one finds that poor students attend schools about as well funded as the ones that non-poor students attend. You also find that schools with high concentrations of black or brown students receive similar funding. In 2008, researchers at the Urban-Brookings Tax Policy Center and the Urban Institute studied the differences between per-student spending in districts serving minority and white students. They found that, "Spending differences have largely disappeared. Spending levels across districts have converged; most remaining differences in spending are between rather than within states."[144] This means that, although you may have some states spending more per student than other states on average, both poor and non-poor students within states receive similar funding.

Georgia, for example, spends roughly $3,000 more per student per year than Idaho. Still, spending between schools within Georgia is similar, regardless of the amount of poor or non-poor students enrolled at any particular school. Wheeler County, one of the poorest in Georgia, has a median household income of $35,400 per year.[145] One of the wealthiest counties in Georgia, Fulton County, has a median household income of $87,605per year – over double that of Wheeler. Yet, the elementary schools in Fulton spend only 7 percent more per student on average each year.[146] Twenty-one of Fulton County elementary schools spend slightly less per student than the elementary school in Wheeler. Even though spending between these counties on children is similar, students in Wheeler test nearly one grade level below the national average, whereas students in Fulton county test at the national average.[147]

We also find achievement disparities in the learning rates of children in Wheeler and Fulton. Learning rates measure how much a given population of children improve their scores while in school and may be a more accurate reflection of a school's quality than average test scores. Test scores can reflect educational opportunities outside of school, such as the number of museums, libraries, or after-school programs a family has access to. By focusing only on how much children are improving while in school, researchers can better differentiate between a school's effectiveness and the contributions of other variables. Children in Wheeler County learn 17 percent less each grade than the U.S. average, whereas children in Fulton County fall only 3 percent behind the U.S. average.[148] The schools in both counties receive similar funding, yet the achievement outcomes of one lag far behind the other, both in average test scores and learning rates. This indicates that, after controlling for out-of-school factors and school funding, the students in Fulton are achieving more than the students in Wheeler.

Demographic differences between student populations often accompany achievement gaps between similarly funded schools. Poor students often have lower levels of academic achievement than non-poor students, so filling a school with a bunch of poor kids is a sure-fire way to lower that school's average reading and math scores. But lumping poor students together in a school can also have a compounding effect. Low-income children in high-poverty schools achieve less than low-income children in low-poverty schools. There is an additional drag on the achievement of schools with high concentrations of poor kids—namely, a chaotic school culture. High-poverty schools generally have significant discipline issues, which negatively affect student learning and teacher effectiveness. These factors make it harder for students attending high-poverty schools to achieve at high levels.

A 2018 nationally representative survey conducted by the Fordham Institute found significant behavioral disparities between high-poverty and low-poverty schools. Teachers in high poverty schools were "more than twice as likely to say that 'verbal disrespect' is a daily occurrence in the classroom. These teachers were more than six times as likely to say that 'physical fighting' is a daily or weekly occurrence in their school, and more than three times as likely to report being personally assaulted by a student."[149] Nearly 60 percent of survey respondents said that "student behavior problems contributed to a disorderly or unsafe environment that made it difficult for many students to learn." One respondent added, "When you have students with behavioral problems in your classroom, it is nearly impossible to teach. You begin to despise your job and want out. If the administration does not back you up 100%, you can chalk up the year as a wash."[150]

Predictably, schools wracked by discipline issues have trouble retaining good teachers. In a 2015 survey conducted by the Denver Classroom Teachers Association, nearly 40 percent of respondents indicated they had considered moving to another school because of discipline issues.[151] Experienced teachers in high-poverty schools are increasingly unable to discipline children appropriately for fear of reprisal. In 2014, the Department of Education advised school districts that they may be prosecuted for violating the Civil Rights Act if different racial groups were disciplined at different rates. President Obama's Secretary of Education, Arne Duncan, had argued that minority children were overrepresented in school discipline data because teachers and administrators were racially discriminatory. He argued that the disparate impact of school discipline on minority children was "not caused by differences in children." It was the "adult behavior that needs to change."[152] This prompted schools to rethink their discipline policies and ensure that different groups of children were equally represented in the discipline data.

Ultimately, this meant that teachers and administrators were pressured to stop disciplining students for fear of reporting numbers that could be interpreted as discriminatory. In high-poverty schools, most of which have high minority enrollments, the effects of such disciplinary regression can be devastating. For example, teachers in Buffalo, NY, have been completely hamstrung in their efforts to get control of their classrooms. When describing their school's discipline issues, one teacher said that "I have never seen anything like it." They added, "The behavior is unreal. The students know that they can get away with acting out because there are no real consequences. The kids are controlling the school – fights, furniture being thrown, students eloping, nonstop verbal abuse/swearing at staff and students."[153] Another teacher described her situation in a different Buffalo school as follows:

"Sexual harassment of teachers and other students is not taken seriously. Nothing is done. Last year I was sexually harassed twice and I was told that the student had problems and that I just had to understand that... A student threw a box of books at me. Nothing was done... It is impossible to go into work every day in an environment like that. I was once a healthy and happy passionate teacher, and now I suffer from PTSD and anxiety and depression and am unable to work... It is impossible to manage behaviors at a 100% poverty school."[154]

The Black/White Achievement Gap

In Escambia County, FL, the average white student is testing nearly 2.5 grade levels higher than the average black student.[155] In August 2021, school Superintendent Dr. Timothy A. Smith attempted to address this gap by mandating that all district staff watch a video to improve their "cultural competency." Apparently, teachers and administrators needed to know just how different black children are. Racism and bias were holding these children back, and only through improving one's cultural competency could truly antiracist educators eradicate the achievement gaps found in Escambia's schools.

The video mandated by Smith began with a store owner harassing black kids. Someone called the cops, and the children scattered. In another scene, a white doctor insinuated that the black child with a broken arm in his office didn't break it skateboarding – he must have been assaulted by his mother at home. Next, a white woman leaves the park with her daughter when a black child and his father arrive to play. The implication is that she wasn't late for any appointments; she just couldn't stand to have her white girl in the same park as a black boy.

The video continued with narrators explaining that students in Escambia were struggling to succeed because they had to contend with "white middle-class norms." Those watching the video learned that black students faced additional barriers that other students did not; low expectations, being taught by Caucasian teachers, and a lack of belonging.

Rather than learning to read, write, and speak according to the universal standard expected of all other students, educators would learn that black children needed to be allowed to use Ebonics in the classroom – the term "Ebonics" was used explicitly. Standard English may be appropriate in some settings, but educators abused black children whenever they suppressed Ebonics in favor of higher standards.

"The student expectations for minority students," one narrator explains, "actually have to be higher than what is considered normal expectations. Because, unfortunately, these students often have to work twice as hard for half as much."[156] This is because, as video viewers would learn, systemic racism was playing an integral part of each child's life inside and outside of the classroom.

To anyone who isn't a Critical Thinker, this video was utterly racist. It painted black children as victims who were incapable of being held to the same high standards as others. Standard English is the international language of business and trade. There is a reason we track children's reading and writing proficiency. Namely, we know mastery of reading and writing will substantially improve a child's chances of getting into the college of their choice and landing in the lucrative career of their dreams. The suggestion that there is a reading proficiency gap between white and black students because Ebonics isn't allowed in the classroom is an absurd display of racism that would once have been made only by the most overt bigots. To suggest that Escambia's educators were holding black children back through conscious or subconscious efforts is to be so enveloped in conspiracy theory as to render oneself completely unable to be trusted with children.

Thousands of educators across the country joined Dr. Timothy A. Smith in his efforts to do something about the achievement gap. By all observable measures, black students are not achieving at the levels of white, Asian, and, increasingly, Hispanic students. Critical Thinkers argue that a lack of cultural competency, funding disparities, and systemic racism cause these gaps. But, as all available evidence suggests, the achievement gaps we see between students are almost entirely a result of familial socioeconomic circumstances.

It is not surprising that the average black child is not achieving at the level of their white and Asian peers. Nearly 7 in 10 black children are born out of wedlock in the United States. That rate is almost triple the out-of-wedlock birth rate for white children and nearly six times that of Asian children. More than half of all black children live in a mother-only household.[157] By comparison, 75 percent of white children and 84 percent of Asian children live with their married parents.[158] Furthermore, only 27 percent of black children live with a parent with a bachelor's degree compared to 53 percent of white children and 69 percent of Asian children.[159] One-third of all black children live in poverty.[160] Only one in ten white and Asian children face the same obstacle.

In short, too many black children are growing up in broken homes. Consequently, too many black children are growing up in poverty. Too many poor children are attending schools where nearly every one of their peers is also poor. These factors are the real drivers of America's achievement gap – not systemic racism. It is absurd to believe that the average child born into the shadow of poverty with only one parent to rely on can be expected to start school as well prepared to learn as the average child born to married parents. It's also absurd to act as if parental education doesn't positively affect a child's achievement. Everyone instantly recognizes these facts when comparing the achievement of white children born to single, uneducated mothers to the achievement of white children born to married and educated parents. Everyone understands that gap. However, Critical Thinkers simply ignore it.

Critical Thinkers also ignore the fact that high-poverty schools are often hampered by discipline issues that diminish teacher effectiveness. Many of these schools have trouble filling vacancies, and it's not because teachers don't want to teach in black and brown classrooms. It's because teachers don't want to deal with harassment, disrespect, physical threats, and violence. Teachers don't enjoy being hamstrung by bloated bureaucracies that refuse to address the real needs of children with behavioral problems –strict disciplinary standards, physically safe learning environments, and extremely high expectations. When these three criteria are met, educators can move mountains.

In Department of Defense (DoDEA) schools, black children achieve at much higher levels than their National Public School (NPS) peers. In 2019, black children in DoDEA schools outscored black NPS children by 25 points on the NAEP 4th grade reading assessment. They also outscored black NPS children by 17 points in math. Furthermore, black children in DoDEA schools performed just a single point lower than their white NPS peers on their 4th-grade NAEP reading assessment and only eight points lower on math. The gaps for those same assessments between black and white NPS children in 2019 were 26 and 25 points, respectively.[161]

The children attending DoDEA schools often qualify for free or reduced-price lunch, and their parents generally have only a high school education. Thirty-five percent of DoDEA students change schools each year. Despite these factors, high student expectations, low tolerance for student misbehavior and discipline issues, and a commitment to excellence propel DoDEA school children to achieve at very high levels.

In New York City (NYC) Charter Schools, black children outperformed not only their black peers in traditional NYC school districts, but they also outperformed their white peers. Black NYC Charter students outscored white NYC District students by 7 percent on their combined 3rd-– 8th-grade English and Language Arts (ELA) assessments. They also outscored white NYC District students by more than 8 percent on their mathematics assessments.

Like DoDEA schools, NYC Charter schools aren't filled with rich white kids. Nearly 80 percent of children attending a NYC Charter school are economically disadvantaged. Ninety percent are either black or Latino. This demographic makeup shatters the idea that high poverty schools with high minority enrollments are destined to fail because white administrators and "white middle-class norms" get in their way. The students in these schools achieve at high levels because educators hold them to high expectations – expectations buttressed by a culture of excellence, community, and discipline.

We know why some kids are more likely to achieve and others are not. It's time we stopped pretending otherwise, chasing phantom allegations of systemic racism in circles while our children suffer the consequences. More children need to be born to married and educated parents for the black and white achievement gap to close. More children need to attend schools where most of their classmates are not poor. More schools need to worry less about how their disciplinary measures may be perceived and more about enforcing school discipline to retain effective teachers and create physically safe learning environments. More schools need to develop cultures of excellence, community, and high expectations. Until parents and educators address these causal factors, we should not expect to witness a significant closure of the black and white achievement gap. Our children deserve better.

CHAPTER SEVEN

EDUCATION DISMANTLED

> "It's high time to remember that our first allegiance is to the human race. And the human race broke away from the animal world through thought and speech. It is natural that these should be free. And if they are shackled—we return to our animal state."
>
> --Aleksandr Solzhenitsyn,
> Open Letter to the Secretariat of
> the RSFSR Writer's Union

Education in the U.S. is now Critical. Children across the country learn that the world is split into two competing factions; those who have power and those who don't. They are learning to essentialize their race. That is to say, they are taught that their skin color means something. They are learning that society forces them into a future that is not of their choosing and that their immutable characteristics predetermine their life outcomes. They are learning that everything must be disrupted and dismantled.

Paul Rossi, formerly a math teacher at Grace Church High School in Manhattan, was kicked out of his classroom for speaking out against the Critical Education he was expected to deliver. In a piece published in April of 2021, Rossi described the "repressive ideology" that had captured his employer.

"My school, like so many others, induces students via shame and sophistry to identify primarily with their race before their individual identities are fully formed. Students are pressured to conform their opinions to those broadly associated with their race and gender and to minimize or dismiss individual experiences that don't match those assumptions. The morally compromised status of "oppressor" is assigned to one group of students based on their immutable characteristics. In the meantime, dependency, resentment and moral superiority are cultivated in students considered 'oppressed'."[162]

At Grace Church High School, parents shell out $50 thousand a year to have their children programmed to practice Critical Thinking. The students, who live in Manhattan, Brooklyn, Queens, the Bronx, and New Jersey, are learning that "objectivity," "individualism," "fear of open conflict," and "a right to comfort" are "characteristics of white supremacy." They learn that racism is systemic, all while attending racially segregated "self-care" meetings.

Critical Thinkers have captured Grace Church High School by using the radical claim that disparities in student outcomes – achievement gaps – are caused by society's underlying systemic power differentials. To achieve equity (equality of outcome), school teachers and administrators map their corrupted moral orthodoxy onto school curriculum, homework, and grading policies. This "Commitment to Antiracism, Equity, and Belonging"[163] is, in practice, a commitment to entrench racism, eliminate real diversity, and exclude anyone who would challenge the new status quo. Students aren't taught how to think. They are taught how they must think.

Before being forced out of a job he loved, several students had approached Rossi, expressing their frustration with the indoctrination at their school.

"They report that, in their classes and other discussions, they must never challenge any of the premises of our 'antiracist' teachings, which are deeply informed by Critical Race Theory. These concerns are confirmed for me when I attend grade-level and all-school meetings about race or gender issues. There, I witness student after student sticking to a narrow script of acceptable responses. Teachers praise insights when they articulate the existing framework or expand it to apply to novel domains. Meantime, it is common for teachers to exhort students who remain silent that 'we really need to hear from you'."[164]

Rossi challenged the Critical dogma of his institution, attempting to "model for students that they should feel safe to question ideological assertions if they felt moved to do so." In a mandatory whites-only Zoom meeting, he challenged the orthodoxy of Critical Thinking by arguing that educators shouldn't racialize human attributes. For that, he was reprimanded. The head of the high school claimed that Rossi had caused "harm" to students.

The indoctrination happening at Grace Church High School is not unique. Other teachers-turned-whistleblowers across the country have revealed how Critical K-12 education has become.

A whistleblower at Westerly School District in Rhode Island revealed training documents that explicitly called for educators to develop a "critical consciousness" in their students. Teachers were told to "empower them [students] to move from critical reflection to critical motivation to critical action so they can transform their lives, communities, and society."[165]

A whistleblower at San Diego Unified School District in California released training documents that accused American educators of the "spirit murdering of Black children."[166] The training literature included a slide that argued, "Whiteness reproduces poverty, failing schools, high unemployment, school closings, and trauma for people of color." "White educators" were blamed for creating and deriving privileges from "white supremacy culture."[167]

The dismantling of K-12 public and private education is unfolding before our very eyes. Whatever banner Critical Thinkers do this under matters not. The various programs all share the same goal; to make Critical Thinkers of America's children.

Pedagogy of the Oppressed

If one had to blame a single text for the corruption of teachers and their classrooms across the country, it would have to be Paulo Freire's *Pedagogy of the Oppressed*.

First published in English in 1970, *Pedagogy of the Oppressed* is now cornerstone reading in most teacher certification programs. In incorporating Freire's ideology, teachers and school administrators reimagine classrooms as political arenas wherein the educator's primary job is to awaken a critical consciousness in their students.

Freire was a neo-Marxist activist who sought to develop a pedagogy (an approach to teaching) of the oppressed that would "produce revolutionary subjects, empowered to overthrow oppression and to create a more democratic and just social order."[168] Rather than seeing education as a means to produce citizens capable of navigating a liberal and democratic society, Freire prescribed a pedagogy that would place educators and students into constant critical dialogue. Education, in his view, was political. It was an exercise in helping students achieve "liberation" by practicing neo-Marxist Critical Theory.

Freire believed that students and educators were, for the most part, not aware of the innumerable ways in which society oppressed them. Educators and students were thought to have a false consciousness – they internalized the dominant values and norms of an oppressive society; so they were blind to their subjugation.

"One of the gravest obstacles to the achievement of liberation is that oppressive reality absorbs those within it and thereby acts to submerge human beings' consciousness. Functionally, oppression is domesticating. To no longer be prey to its force, one must emerge from it and turn upon it. This can be done only by means of the praxis: reflection and action upon the world in order to transform it." – Paulo Freire, *Pedagogy of the Oppressed*

To break this false consciousness, curriculum, lessons, and classroom dialogue must be Critical. That is to say, everything the teacher and students do must involve a Critical "praxis" – the practice of Critical Theory.

According to Freire, teachers are at the forefront of the oppressive educational system. This system indoctrinates children into the "myths created and developed in the old order, which like specters haunt the new structure emerging from the revolutionary transformation."[169] To liberate themselves and their students, teachers must "authentically commit" to the struggle for liberation and "re-examine themselves constantly" for how they reproduce oppression in their classrooms.

In this context, reproducing oppression happens when educators feed dominant sociopolitical and cultural norms to students through traditional teaching methods. This traditional process is thought to adapt students to the oppressive system, manipulating their ability to understand the true nature of the society they live in. In other words, educators are hiding the possibility of freedom from their students when they use traditional teaching methods.

When teachers use assignments, grades, and standardized tests, they judge their students against the "general configuration of a "good, organized, and just"" society; they are critiquing students against false moral standards to situate them forever into the oppressed class. This, according to neo-Marxists like Freire, was a cycle that must be dismantled.

"Manipulation, like the conquest whose objectives it serves, attempts to anesthetize the people so they will not think. For if the people join to their presence in the historical process critical thinking about that process, the threat of their emergence materializes in revolution. Whether one calls this correct thinking "revolutionary consciousness" or "class consciousness," it is an indispensable precondition of revolution." – Freire, *Pedagogy of the Oppressed*

Several generations of teachers and school administrators have been taught to view and practice teaching as the revolutionary struggle Freire thought it to be. Academic journals like *Educational Administration Quarterly* regularly publish the works of highly influential, Freire-inspired activists. Consider the 2008 publication *From the Field: A Proposal for Educating Leaders for Social Justice*, in which prominent educators write:

"This development of critical consciousness in prospective leaders must be embedded throughout the educational preparation program, including integrating these intentions into all recruitment and selection materials; within student orientation; within student advising; and throughout course work, course assessments, and program assessments."[170]

Today, academics and educators combine Freire's ideas with other Critical and Postmodern Theories to practice Critical Pedagogy – a method of teaching sometimes described as "Culturally Relevant Pedagogy," "Culturally Relevant Teaching," "Antiracist Education," "Transformative Social-Emotional Learning," or "Critical Race Methodology."

This new theory of teaching has become the cornerstone of contemporary K-12 education.

Critical Pedagogy

Critical Pedagogy incorporates many critical and postmodern theories, but one has been incorporated more than any other; Critical Race Theory (CRT).

Critical Race Theory was developed by disgruntled students and academics who thought an earlier movement, Critical Legal Studies (CLS), wasn't a specific enough tool to generate social change. This earlier CLS movement had applied the neo-Marxist

Antonio Gramsci's idea of hegemony to law, attempting to explain how "legal ideology has helped create, support, and legitimate America's present class structure."[171] However, this movement had failed to account for race and did not provide "pragmatic strategies for material social transformation."[172]

Early CRT scholars were trying to theorize the shortcomings of constitutional law and the civil rights movement. These activists argued that legal scholarship and laws were fundamentally racial and, therefore, race was *the lens* through which one should view and interpret societal structures.

The Critical Race Theory (CRT) movement is described, by founding Critical Race Theorists, as "a collection of activists and scholars interested in studying and transforming the relationship among race, racism and power."[173] The first wave of Critical Race Theorists did not think that the Civil Rights movement had gone far enough in redressing the injustices of slavery and Jim Crow in the United States. They also believed that racism hadn't improved since the passage of the Civil Rights Act in 1964. Instead, Critical Race Theorists argued that liberalism merely camouflaged the rampant injustice and discrimination that was still taking place all around them. CRT was a vehicle for addressing this problem and prescribing revolutionary action.

Like all critical theories, activism is a foundational element of CRT.

"Unlike some academic disciplines, critical race theory contains an activist dimension. It not only tries to understand our social situation, but to change it; it sets out not only to ascertain how society organizes itself along racial lines and hierarchies, but to transform it for the better"[174]

There are several tenets of Critical Race Theory that nearly all Critical Race Theorists agree upon. First, Critical Race Theorists argue that racism is permanent and will never go away. It is "ordinary, not aberrational –normal science, the usual way society does business, the common, everyday experience of most people of color in this country."[175]

Secondly, Critical Race Theorists argue that liberalism is an insufficient framework for addressing the permanence of racism. As Jean Stefancic and Richard Delgado, two of the world's most prominent Critical Race Theorists, write in *Critical Race Theory: An Introduction:*

"Unlike traditional civil rights, which embraces incrementalism and step-by-step progress, critical race theory questions the very foundations of the liberal order, including equality theory, legal reasoning, Enlightenment rationalism, and neutral principles of constitutional law."[176]

Third, Critical Race Theorists use the theory of intersectionality to diagnose how systemic power can influence one's overlapping identities. That is to say, Critical Race Theorists argue that none of us have a unitary perspective from which we can critique society. Rather, we can subdivide our "positionality" along the lines of race, sex, gender, ability, class, and every other conceivable dimension to understand the multitudinous ways in which we are oppressed.

Fourth, Critical Race Theorists anchor subjectivity in "voices of color" and "counter-storytelling." Here, the postmodern influence is undeniable. Rather than reaching for objective criteria to judge someone's assertion, Critical Race Theorists argue that "minority status... brings with it a presumed competence to speak about race and racism."[177] This means Critical Race Theorists regularly reinterpret historical events and contemporary situations, engineering new meaning to suit their ideological commitments.

Lastly, Critical Race Theorists universally argue that "whiteness is property." In short, Critical Race Theorists believe societal privileges and benefits are granted to those that are white or "act white." As Robin DiAngelo and Ozlem Sensory write in their book, *Is Everyone Really Equal?: An Introduction to Key Concepts in Social Justice Education*:

"Critical scholars define *racism* as a systemic relationship of unequal power between White people and people of Color. *Whiteness* refers to the specific dimensions of racism that elevate White people over people of Color. Basic rights, resources, and experiences that are assumed to be shared by all, are actually only available to Whites."

In short, CRT maintains that the current liberal democratic order is saturated with a permanent racism that will never go away. This racism is camouflaged in liberal ideas like equality of opportunity and merit. Dominant groups use liberal institutions and hidden racism to force marginalized groups into predetermined situations and outcomes. To find this racism, Critical Race Theorists are needed; they are trained to critique societal structures and to use their unique knowledge and voice to find racism. Once found, "aggressive, color-conscious efforts"[178] are needed to secure equality of outcomes; equity is prescribed to redistribute power and privilege in order to combat whiteness.

For three decades, educators across the country have incorporated the presuppositions and tenets of Critical Race Theory into their Critical Pedagogy. Expanding the practice of Critical Race Theory into the classroom was a "logical extension of the work."[179]

In 1995, Gloria Ladson-Billings and William F. Tate IV released an article titled *Toward a Critical Race Theory of Education* that would popularize CRT and catalyze a fundamental change in K-12 education. Billings and Tate argued that "race was *the* central construct for understanding inequality." They believed the persistent achievement gap between white, black, and brown children might be closed by injecting classrooms with CRT.

The central argument of this early work was that whiteness is a socially constructed "normative" category against which all students are compared: "In a racialized society where whiteness is positioned as normative, *everyone* is ranked and categorized in relation to these points of opposition."[180]

Critical Race Theorists believe that whiteness is a set of customs, cultural beliefs, standards, and norms that constitute the white racialized identity. Critical Race Theorists argue that whiteness is the standard by which society categorizes things as good, bad, just, or normal. In their view, it is as if society has a barcode scanner that only allows those with a whiteness card to pass through certain checkpoints and doors. Whiteness is the "ultimate property"[181]; a capital that white people receive interest payments on in the form of unearned benefits and privileges (which are known collectively as "white privilege").

Gloria Ladson-Billings explicitly makes this argument in her 1998 paper *Just what is critical race theory and what's it doing in a nice field like education?*. She writes, "Conceptual categories like 'school achievement,' 'middle classness,' 'maleness,' 'beauty,' 'intelligence,' and 'science' become normative categories of whiteness." In other words, Billings claims that when we think about things like "middle classness" and "school achievement," we only picture what those things look like from a white perspective. The argument is that this perspective is thought to be "correct."Therefore, any other perspective is believed to be "false." Society won't accept those perspectives as "good" ways of acting and "being" in society.

For Critical Race Theorists, the K-12 educational system "centers" whiteness; it holds whiteness in the highest regard, rewarding those teachers and students who are in proximity to it. That is to say, Critical Race Theorists maintain that curriculum, instruction, and grading policies are all designed with whiteness in mind. Critical Race Theorists claim that academic achievement isn't about achievement at all – it is merely a way to categorize: which students are close to whiteness and which are not; which students are doing what society expects of them and which are not; and which students are "good" and which are "bad". This is the presupposition from which Critical Educators begin practicing Critical Pedagogy.

Dismantling Excellence

"Although CRT began as a movement in the law, it has rapidly spread beyond that discipline. Today, many in the field of education consider themselves critical race theorists who use CRT's ideas to understand issues of school discipline and hierarchy, tracking, controversies over curriculum and history, and IQ and achievement testing." – Richard Delgado and Jean Stefancic, *Critical Race Theory: An Introduction*

Critical Educators have applied Critical Race Theory to education for at least 25 years. Many teachers in the U.S. are now convinced that their primary responsibility as educators is to use their classroom as a means to achieve Critical Social Justice. These Critical Educators have adopted a pedagogy of the oppressed. They see their students as products of an unjust society, products that must be broken down and reassembled in accordance with postmodern neo-Marxist theories of identity. Critical Race Theory is one of the tools these Critical Educators use to achieve this end.

Critical Educators take concrete measures to disrupt and dismantle their classrooms. The most egregious of these are the curriculum transformations, the condemnation of meritocracy, and the devaluing or elimination of grading policies and standardized tests.

Critical Curriculum

Critical Race Theorists have long argued that an "official school curriculum" is a "culturally specific artifact designed to maintain a White supremacist master script."[182] Critical Educators believe they must dismantle the curriculum as a means of breaking society's codified whiteness. A traditional curriculum is seen as a method for suppressing the critical consciousness their students will need to authentically navigate the world. By radically transforming their curriculum, Critical Educators lead their students to liberation.

We find an example of this radical transformation in *A Pathway to Equitable Math Instruction*, an 82-page workbook that helps Critical Educators deconstruct "racism in mathematics."[183] As the workbook explains, "In order to embody antiracist math education, teachers must engage in critical praxis that interrogates the ways in which they perpetuate white supremacy culture in their own classrooms."[184]

According to the workbook, characteristics of this white supremacy culture are – perfectionism; a sense of urgency; defensiveness; the worship of the written word; either/or thinking; power hoarding; individualism; the belief in only one right way; objectivity; and a right to comfort.[185]

The workbook is broken down into a calendar. Each month has a specific action step Critical Educators must take to dismantle white supremacy in their curriculum and classroom activities. January's call-to-action is to remove the "forced construct of linear teaching" because it "reinforces objectivity."[186] September's call-to-action is to stop tracking students into different math courses because that perpetuates the "notion that adults know what the right thing is for them."[187] By tracking students into a lower course because they have not mastered the foundational concepts of algebra, educators are "reinforcing paternalism and powerhoarding."[188]

This workbook was produced with funding from the Bill and Melinda Gates Foundation and is accompanied by additional online courses and resources. Critical Educators across the country use it to develop and implement their antiracist math policies.

Another example of educators transforming their curriculum is the situating of *The 1619 Project* as a cornerstone of U.S. history.

The 1619 Project is a New York Times publication that attempts to fundamentally change the founding narrative of the United States. *The 1619 Project's* central claim is that the 13 colonies in North America declared independence from Great Britain because they wanted to protect the institution of slavery. Nikole Hannah-Jones, lead author of the project, argues that Great Britain was enveloped in a conversation that would see slavery abolished. This, Jones claimed, was the impetus for the founding fathers to draft a Declaration of Independence.

With this radical claim established, *The 1619 Project* construes all of American history as black vs. white and oppressed vs. oppressor. While it is demonstrably true that racism and slavery have been central to the American story, it is equally untrue that racism and slavery have defined the American experiment. It is an outright lie that the founding fathers went to war to protect the institution of slavery.

Dozens of historians have critiqued *The 1619 Project*, bringing to bear its numerous inaccuracies. *The 1619 Project* argues that slavery was uniquely American – which it wasn't. Slavery was a worldwide phenomenon. According to the Trans-Atlantic Slave Trade Database, of the 12.5 million Africans that were shipped out of Africa, only 3 percent were sent directly to North America.[189] *The 1619 Project* also maintained that the Founding Fathers weren't embroiled in a bitter debate about the institution of slavery – which they were. Thomas Jefferson included an entire passage in an earlier draft of the Declaration of Independence denouncing the King of England for waging "cruel war against human nature itself, violating its most sacred rights of life and liberty in the persons of a distant people who never offended him, captivating and carrying them into slavery in another hemisphere or to incur miserable death in their transportation thither."[190]

The most inaccurate thing about The 1619 Project is perhaps not a factual error but a crucial, and telling omission. *The 1619 Project* doesn't acknowledge that the Declaration of Independence sealed the fate of slavery in what would become the United States of America. The American experiment was the first of its kind; an experiment that brought slavery into question at the very moment of its conception, guaranteeing inalienable rights of life, liberty, and the pursuit of happiness for all. The country struggled with this, and much of U.S. history is abhorrent – like much of the history of all human beings. But the West, and America specifically, set the world on a path to eradicate a practice that had existed for thousands of years. How the writers could leave that out is beyond comprehension unless we understand that the purpose isn't to get the history right. The objective is to manipulate it, to delegitimize a country and develop a critical mass of students with a critical consciousness.

Critical Educators have latched on to *The 1619 Project* as a practice of counter-storytelling, a way to delegitimize what they consider to be an unjust and color-blind liberal order. As of May 2020, more than 3,500 schools have used materials based on *The 1619 Project* across various grade levels. Critical Educators teach these children to use race as *the lens* through which they must consume, interpret, and understand American history.

Many other curriculum changes are happening around the country. In 2021, Christopher F. Rufo, a writer and filmmaker turned investigative journalist, broke into the mainstream political discourse for his reporting on the widespread implementation of Critical Pedagogy and CRT in K-12 education. With whistleblower documents, Rufo revealed just how Critical education has become.

In Cupertino, California, 3rd-grade students "deconstruct their racial and sexual identities" and "rank themselves according to their power and privilege" by completing "identity maps" in their classroom. These students learn that "a white, cisgender man, who is able-bodied, heterosexual, considered handsome and speaks English has more privilege than a Black transgender woman."[191]

In Philadelphia, 5th-grade students celebrate "black communism" and "simulate a Black Power rally to "Free Angela Davis" from prison." (Angela Davis was openly a communist for decades and studied under Herbert Marcuse.)

In Buffalo, teachers are told that they must "be woke, which is basically critically conscious." They are to begin "preparing them at four years old" to be "activists for antiracism." Children must learn "Black Lives Matter principles," which include "dismantling cisgender privilege," creating "queer-affirming network[s] where heteronormative thinking no longer exists," and "the disruption of Western nuclear family dynamics."[192]

In North Carolina's largest school district, teachers are told that "You can't let parents deter you from the work." If parents have a problem with the district's new "transformational interventions" to disrupt whiteness in the classroom, teachers are instructed to "have the confidence to take risks and make difficult decisions that are rooted in their values."[193]

Educational Equity

It is not enough for Critical Educators to disrupt and dismantle their curriculum. They are also working to dismantle gifted programs, grading policies, and standardized tests in the name of equity.

Gifted programs and specialized schools are used to challenge children with above-average or exceptional ability; to capitalize on a student's strengths and make sure they encounter sufficient amounts of academic rigor to meet their skill level. These programs and schools require that a student has demonstrated high levels of academic proficiency before admitting a student, as measured by standardized tests and GPA. They are overwhelmingly merit-based.

Critical Educators hate these programs because they are not "diverse" enough. Specifically, there are too many white and Asian students in them.

Although the black and white achievement gap receives the most attention, the largest achievement gap in education is between Asian American students and everyone else. Asian American students surpass all other groups on the National Assessment for Educational Progress in mathematics and reading. They dominate the SAT, have greater college admission rates, and have higher levels of degree attainment.

This level of academic excellence leads to a disproportionate share of Asian American children in gifted programs and specialized schools across the country. Asian Americans dominate elite high schools that use specialized tests to filter highly competitive talent pools. At Brooklyn Tech, one of New York City's most prestigious charter schools, Asian American students make up 61 percent of the student population.

This is a massive problem for Critical Thinkers. If white and Asian Americans are overrepresented, then other groups of students must be underrepresented. Critical Thinkers find this intolerable, seeing it as a situation that only perpetuates unequal outcomes (inequities) between children. If standardized tests and grades are being used to fast-track students into specialized programs and schools, those tools must be dismantled.

The easiest way to dismantle grades and standardized tests is to eliminate them. Educators at Thomas Jefferson High School for Science and Technology in Fairfax, VA, recently scrapped their admissions test. U.S. News & World Report rates this school as the nation's number one public high school. When the changes took effect, Asian American representation at the school plummeted, from 75 percent to 54 percent.

In February of 2021, the San Francisco Board of Education voted to end its merit-based admissions policy at Lowell High School. The data isn't yet available to measure a change, but Asian Americans represented 50 percent of the school's population when the votes were cast.[194]

In October of 2021, NYC Mayor Bill De Blasio unveiled a plan to "replace the highly selective program [Gifted and Talented Program], which has become a glaring symbol of segregation in New York City public schools."

Like the parents of Asian American students in Virginia and California, Asian American parents in NYC knew what these changes meant. They meant that their children might not have a chance to attend accelerated programming, no matter how hard they worked. These parents knew that Critical Educators would thus be discriminating against their children.

The Chinese American Citizens Alliance of Greater New York responded to De Blasio's plan with a scathing press release on October 10, 2021.

"Dumbing down for 'equity' is a nationwide plague. Calculus classes are canceled from high schools because of 'diversity': 'too many' Asian and White students. Algebra classes are banned from middle schools because Black students are not 'included' in them. In elementary schools, rigorous Math is replaced by 'culturally responsive', 'inquiry-based' Math to fit students "lived experiences," i.e. learning to do Math is replaced by Math appreciation.

"We are arguing against shadows: taking away G&T is not about education, which the woke are obviously dumbing down. It's about 'equity,' which means equal outcomes in CRT. And you don't get to equal outcomes by expanding opportunities under equal rights, i.e. by adding more programs; you get to equal outcomes by taking away.

"If you nourish the lawn, all grass will grow better but not to equal heights; if you mow the lawn, all grass will be equally short. The woke's education arguments are covers for CRT. And CRT is about racial retribution: to take things away from Whites, to punish Whites for privilege. The goal is for Whites to lose, even if Blacks aren't helped, and Asians be damned."[195]

From East to West, districts across the country are dismantling what they consider to be "segregation" programs. In California, millions of students could be affected by this effort. Critical Educators are on the verge of eliminating all tracking programs in math before the 10th grade. This means that Critical Educators will force all students to learn mathematics at the same pace until they reach high school, regardless of proficiency. If a child is ready for Algebra 1 in 7th grade, too bad. They must be left to their own devices, swamped by perpetual boredom in an environment designed to grind their love of mathematics out of their bones in the name of social justice.

Classrooms across the country are no longer penalizing students for turning in late work. Many no longer use traditional grading scales. The explicit goal is to equalize educational outcomes among children. This won't happen naturally, because children are diverse; they have different interests, abilities, intelligence, work ethics, and barriers. They come from different homes with different family structures, values, and social environments; and they also come from different cultures, religions, and geographies.

Equity and diversity are irreconcilable. One cannot have a diverse classroom and, at the same time, expect to measure equal outcomes among students. This can only be achieved by using the most superficial form of diversity – diversity of skin color and gender; a form of diversity which, in this context, is a fundamentally racist and sexist idea. To assume gifted programs are not diverse because students within them don't constitute a representative share of the overall population's skin color and sex is to assume one knows what a student thinks by looking at them; to assume that their skin color or gender can tell you anything at all about them.

In the last chapter, I discussed the importance of excellence and structure in education. Education has always been a way for kids from disadvantaged backgrounds to equalize the playing field. Tens of thousands of poor kids across the country are excelling in educational environments that expect nothing less than their best effort. These environments offer rigorous curriculum, difficult assessment, and constant challenge. If it weren't for these environments, these disadvantaged kids might never be able to demonstrate their unique talents, work ethics, or abilities in a manner that could one day lift them out of poverty. By eliminating concrete benchmarks and meritocratic learning environments, Critical Educators are damning the very students they purport to help.

What CRT Is Actually Doing In A Nice Field Like Education

The implementation of Critical Pedagogy and Critical Race Theory in classrooms is not only antithetical to liberalism – it's actually a form of child abuse.

One of the principal tenets of CRT is the theory of intersectionality. When Critical Educators teach intersectionality, they ask students to map out their intersecting social identities to determine where they land on the power and privilege hierarchy. Critical Educators teach children that they must identify by their race, skin color, religion, sexual orientation, family structure, and other characteristics to understand which identities make them oppressors and which make them oppressed. The point is to get students to buy into the idea that the world is all about power and oppressive systems. It is to make students internalize the belief that their identity is one comprised of these oppressor and oppressed dynamics. By making students define themselves as oppressors or oppressed, Critical Educators are forcing them into an untenable situation via mental manipulation, a situation that we are told can only be resolved by following the dictates of the Critical Educator.

Critical Educators coerce students into viewing the world as a zero-sum game in which structures and forces they cannot fully understand predetermine their life outcomes. They are encouraged to ignore the values of their parents and are taught that hard work, equality of opportunity, and merit are bigoted slogans of an immoral, unfair liberal order. Critical Educators teach kids that the practice of politics is inseparable from education; the point isn't only to critique the world but to change it. These children are taught not only what to think – they are taught how to think by requiring them to practice their Critical Thinking skills.

The explicit point of a Critical Education is to break a child's mind. Critical Educators coerce black children into thinking this world is not for them; that society's understanding of them is skin deep; that they must think and act a certain way to be "authentically" or "politically" black; that they are perpetually entrenched in a revolutionary struggle to throw off the yoke of a phantom force that will follow them to the grave.

Critical Educators coerce white children into thinking that the only important thing about them is that they were born with original sin; a stamp representing the sins of long-dead men with whom they have never had any relations. Critical Educators tell white children that the guilt and shame of this original sin is perpetual and that they will forever be cast in a negative light. They are taught that the melanin levels in their skin are indicative of the worst atrocities the world has ever seen.

Critical Educators teach Hispanic children, especially those that are "white-passing," that they too are beneficiaries of whiteness. These children are taught that they have unearned and systemic advantages over other identity groups by being in proximity to whiteness.

Critical Educators teach Asian children that white people use them to drive a racial wedge between oppressed groups. They are taught that the reason why Asian Americans are so successful in the U.S. is because white people have removed systemic barriers to hold up a "model minority" to other racial groups; it is seen as a way of saying, "See! The system is fair. Get your act in order." In other words, Critical Educators teach Asian children that they are nothing more than a racial pawn used to defend a corrupt system.

Critical Educators are deliberately dismantling the minds of American children. They are grooming children to become foot soldiers. What will the next 20 years look like when a generation of children enters adulthood with hyper-racialized identities and a thirst for power? What happens when these children are programmed to become radical revolutionaries? If we do not stop the Woke Warpath rampaging through our schools, we risk raising a generation of children that think of themselves as hammers being held hostage by a society of nails.

CHAPTER EIGHT

WOMEN

"And the simple step of a simple courageous man is not to partake in falsehood, not to support false actions!"

–Aleksandr Solzhenitsyn, Nobel Lecture in Literature 1970

In 2014, Google's Senior Vice President of People Operations, Laszlo Bock, published Google's first annual diversity report. "We've always been reluctant to publish numbers about the diversity of our workforce at Google," he wrote. "We now realize we were wrong, and that it's time to be candid about the issues."[196]

He revealed that, although women made up 50 percent of the population, they only represented 30 percent of all Googlers (Google employees). What's worse, women were even less represented among Google's lucrative technical positions. Only 2 percent of Google's employees were black, and only 3 percent were Hispanic.

Other Silicon Valley giants were also being "candid" about this issue at the time. Facebook's Global Head of Diversity, Maxine Williams, posted her company's diversity data shortly after Bock released his. In a post titled "Building a More Diverse Facebook," Williams wrote that "As these numbers show, we have more work to do – a lot more."[197]

Joining the fray, Apple CEO Tim Cook published his company's data. "Let me say up front: As CEO, I'm not satisfied with the numbers on this page. They're not new to us, and we've been working hard for quite some time to improve them."[198]

At the time when Silicon Valley released its first volley of diversity data, radical movements that made inequality the preeminent issue of our times were dominating the popular political discourse in the U.S. For instance, Occupy Wall Street demonstrators were displaying their disgust with the levels of wealth inequality and corruption modern capitalist economies allowed. Black Lives Matter protestors were demanding that America value black lives as equally as any other. Feminists were demanding equal representation and pay.

Against the backdrop of such movements, Critical Social Justice Ideology rose to prominence as the de-facto political orthodoxy of nearly every mainstream American institution. This new orthodoxy demanded data that proved everyone was being treated equally. The singular metric by which Critical Thinkers evaluated equality was whether or not various identity groups were proportionally represented in any given data set. Women were underrepresented at companies like Google, and Critical Thinkers demanded answers.

Google attributed the lack of women's representation in its workforce to the fact that recruiting and retaining women was difficult. Google simply didn't have a large enough pool of qualified women with backgrounds in computer science to draw from. But Critical Thinkers wouldn't tolerate that explanation. They attributed the lack of women in tech to a system of oppression they call the patriarchy.

For Critical Thinkers, the patriarchy is a system that generates socially constructed power for men that society institutionalizes over women. That is to say; they believe society is built to afford men privileges and power that women do not have. It is as if men have a special access card that grants them admission to better jobs, higher wages, and more respect.

The idea is that society has stamped men with the attributes of strength, confidence, and leadership. Women are considered to be the opposite of men. Women have been stamped as fragile, unsure of themselves, and unable to cope with large amounts of stress.

In this system of patriarchy, a double standard emerges. When a woman acts in a way in which only a "man" is socially allowed to act, society deems her "bitchy" or "bossy." Whereas a man can be considered a natural leader, women can only be considered nurturing followers. When they are devoted to a job, society considers men "go-getters" while women are looked down upon for not spending more time with their children.

The patriarchy is something altogether different to a personal gender stereotype. If a man assumes a woman can't do a "man's job," that man is guilty of gender stereotyping. The idea of the patriarchy is the idea that these gender stereotypes are baked into society itself. This means that women can be the victims of oppression regardless of whether a single gender stereotype is mentioned or acted upon. Society itself is responsible for stereotyping.

A room with no men in it can be said to victimize women because the room was built by people that have been socialized into this patriarchal system. Whether it's the name of the conference room, the types of beverages in the cooler, or the language found in an operational manual, Critical Thinkers believe that everything in this room has been constructed to privilege male access at the expense of women.

The idea that Google can oppress women without a single instance of overt stereotyping is a profound one. This means that if Google could snap its fingers and magically eliminate all workers who hold gender stereotypes, the company could still be oppressing women. Critical Thinkers argue that the patriarchy is an ever-present and inescapable force that shapes all institutions (much like systemic racism). It's not as if Google had been caught overtly denying qualified jobs or promotions to female candidates in 2014. So what explained the gender gap? The hidden patriarchal system was to blame, and, of course, trained Critical Thinkers were needed to disrupt and dismantle it.

Google hired Critical Thinkers to offer "bias busting" workshops in the years following the publication of their first diversity report. By doing the work and educating themselves, Googlers could tackle their unconscious bias and acknowledge their unearned societal privilege in the workplace.

Frame Shift Consulting, "The leader in ally skills training," provided the backbone of Google's bias-busting methodology. In the "Ally Skills Workshop," participants were expected to learn and internalize the definitions of specific terms – oppression, privilege, intersectionality, and power. These terms are taken directly from Critical Social Justice literature, and participants were expected to accept that these definitions and theories, along with their resulting socio-political implications, are true. If a participant disagreed with any of the workshop facilitator's ideological or political stances, they were to be removed. If the facilitator did not remove them, they might start "reproducing oppression inside your workshop."[199]

The Ally Skills Workshop not only calls for attendees to learn about Critical Social Justice Ideology – it calls on them to act. Employees are to "treat ally actions as bare minimum expectations." When such Critical Social Justice Ideology is based on the works and activism of people like Gloria Jean Watkins (who writes as "bell hooks") and Angela Davis, this is cause for concern. Both of these women were radically anti-capitalist and avowed Marxists, Angela Davis having been a member of the Communist Party, who at one point ended up on the FBI's ten most wanted list. When Davis once said, "We will have to destroy the American capitalist system," she was not mincing words. Ultimately, when Google offers unconscious bias training, there is a lot of ideological baggage that comes with it – ideological baggage that demands adherence to Critical Social Justice Ideology and the political activism which follows.

After attending one such workshop, Google senior software engineer James Damore wrote the now-infamous "Google Memo." Whereas Google had concluded that their gender gap stemmed from an unconsciously sexist workforce, and that this sexism was built into the very bedrock of America, Damore argued that much of it could be better explained by the "differences in distributions of traits between men and women."[200] Damore argued that Google had committed itself so strongly to the explanation that sexism must be causing its workforce disparities that the company would no longer tolerate any other explanation or suggestion, regardless of any evidence that might mount up against them.

Damore worried that the company's political leanings and bias had "equated freedom from offense with psychological safety" and that this had led to internal bullying and censorship. "This silencing..." he explained, "has created an ideological echo chamber where some ideas are too sacred to be honestly discussed." Indeed. After the Google Memo went public, Google fired James Damore for "advancing harmful gender stereotypes."[201]

The idea that women are underrepresented in the tech industry because of a universal system of patriarchy and oppression is a radical claim. By convincing everyone that representational differences between groups are inherently a product of discrimination, Critical Thinkers have assumed incredible institutional control. They have bullied their way into positions of power – namely, lucrative DEI (Diversity, Equity, Inclusion) administrative functions – by accusing organizations of upholding misogynistic and racist cultures. With this power, Critical Thinkers have established new workplace rules that create homogenous and exclusionary workforces by silencing dissenting opinions and drawing boundaries around what is and isn't allowed to be said. Google didn't fire James Damore for advancing harmful gender stereotypes. Google fired him for opposing the radical claims of Critical Thinkers.

This chapter first explores why it isn't surprising that women aren't more represented in the tech industry. We will then examine why women might be less represented in other industries. Finally, we study the earnings gap between men and women. In all three cases, we discover that the differences between men's and women's career choices and earnings are best explained by differences in average trait distributions between the two groups – not a conspiratorial patriarchal system. That is to say, we expose the radical claims of Critical Thinkers.

Biology and Personality Influence Career Choices

In the Google Memo, James Damore argued that men and women, on average, are different. He reasoned that gender is not entirely a social construct and that men and women are distinct biological sexes that behave and interact with society in slightly different ways. This means that men and women may have different career preferences and values, which could easily translate into gender gaps in the labor force – gaps that are not the result of discrimination.

Men and women have distinct biological characteristics that affect their behavior. One way scientists study these behavioral differences is by observing infant boys and girls as they play with toys. Children are ideal observational subjects because they have had less time to be socialized into gendered roles, meaning any behavioral differences between the two sexes in infancy are more likely to result from biological variation.

Several studies have shown that infant boys prefer to play with different toys to infant girls. Boys prefer more masculine toys, whereas girls prefer more feminine toys, and this has been demonstrated in infants that are fresh out of the womb. At 24 hours old, there clearly isn't much room for the development of socially constructed gendered norms.

In their first year of life, boys choose to play with trucks more often than girls, and girls choose to play with dolls more often than boys. In a meta-analysis of 16 studies that observed the toy preferences of boys and girls, researchers found that these toy preferences are cross-cultural.[202] If gender were entirely a social construct, one would expect to find that the toy preferences of girls and boys in the United States would differ greatly from those found in Scandinavia, Israel, or China, between which vast societal, institutional, and cultural differences are observed. The scientific literature indicates that, even after accounting for the "presence or absence of an adult, the study setting, the gender equality status of the country... and presence of gender-neutral toys"[203], these preferential differences remained.

Prenatal hormone exposure is probably the driver of such universal observations. Both male and female fetuses are exposed to different concentrations of testosterone during their development. For boys, an increasing concentration of testosterone is associated with a cascade of changes that affect the organization and sexual differentiation of the brain. These changes have an enduring influence on brain development and behavior, ultimately leading to more masculinization.

Knowing this, one might expect that if a girl were exposed to higher concentrations of male sex hormones during fetal development, that girl's behaviors would more closely reflect the masculine behavior of boys. Girls with congenital adrenal hyperplasia (CAH), a condition that exposes them to the overproduction of adrenal androgens (male sex hormones) prenatally, prefer more masculine toys, playmates, and activities, just as one might expect. The higher the level of prenatal adrenal androgen exposure, the stronger the correlation. Likewise, girls with CAH are typically less empathetic and more aggressive than other girls, much like young boys.

The effects of prenatal testosterone on the organization and development of the brain are not specific to the human species.

When female rodents and non-human primates are exposed to higher testosterone levels, they become predictably more masculine too. When male rats are castrated neonatally, they behave more like female rats. Like humans, these behavioral changes are associated with different toy preferences. Male rhesus monkeys strongly prefer wheeled toys, whereas female rhesus monkeys strongly prefer plush toys.[204]

The biological differences between the human sexes not only affect what we like to play with, but they also drive personality trait differences between men and women. In the Google Memo, Damore claimed that women have more "openness directed towards feelings and aesthetics rather than ideas." In "Men and Things, Women and People: A Meta-Analysis of Sex Differences and Interests," researchers cite dozens of studies that back this claim. According to the meta-analysis, "Generally, women are more likely than men to indicate interest in social and artistic activities, whereas men are more likely than women to indicate interest in scientific, technical, and mechanical activities."[205] The paper also importantly notes that, "Lack of interest in the STEM fields or finding other fields to be more interesting is also the top reason given for women switching out of the STEM majors and jobs."[206]

It should be no surprise then that men are drawn to engineering. The entire purpose of an engineer is to work with and obsess over things. One should expect that, although men and women at the center of the people-things trait distribution will vary in their preference for people and things only slightly, the tails of the curve will tell an entirely different story. That is to say, if men generally prefer working with things a bit more than women do, then men on the far tail of the distribution are drastically more likely to prefer working with things over people. They are thus considerably more likely to take up engineering.

Perhaps the most controversial of Damore's claims was that women also have higher anxiety and lower stress tolerance that Damore says "may contribute to the higher levels of anxiety women report on Googlegeist [Google's annual employee survey] and to the lower number of women in high-stress jobs."This declaration is also backed by solid scientific literature.

In one study, researchers examined 37 countries for gender differences related to Eysenck's three personality traits. The strongest finding of that study was that, in all 37 countries, women were, on average, more neurotic than men.[207] The results were consistent cross-culturally and across the socio-economic spectrum. It didn't matter if it was the United States, Bulgaria, China, Egypt, Israel, Nigeria, or Yugoslavia – women were, in varying degrees, more tense and anxious. This evidence directly contradicts the predictions of Critical Thinkers, who argue that, because all differences in behavior between men and women are socially constructed, one would not expect to find universal differences between men and women across continents, countries, cultures, and classes.

Gender Equal Countries Have Larger Gender Gaps

Critical Thinkers claim that, as societies become more egalitarian, gender gaps vanish. That is to say, we should expect that the most gender-equal societies should have the smallest gender gaps. More gender equality means more freedom of choice and empowerment for women to choose what they want to do. If women have complete freedom to choose to work in technical fields in the most gender-equal societies, we should therefore expect equal representation between men and women in those fields.

In the Google Memo, James Damore wrote that "contrary to what a social constructionist would argue, research suggests that "greater nation-level gender equality leads to psychological dissimilarity in men's and women's personality traits." "As society becomes more prosperous and more egalitarian," he continued, "innate dispositional differences between men and women have more space to develop and the gap that exists between men and women in their personality traits becomes wider." We need to stop assuming that gender gaps imply sexism."

The World Economic Forum ranks Iceland, Norway, Sweden, and Finland as the most gender-equal societies in the world. In these countries, bolstered by strong welfare states, women are best situated to make the types of life and career decisions that are most suitable to their interests and aspirations. In Iceland, there is a universal childcare policy, allowing women to overcome the disadvantage of a disproportionate burden of childbearing. In Norway, gender quota legislation dictates that women must represent at least 40 percent of business boards. In Sweden, women hold just as many ministerial positions as men, and in Finland, women hold 42 percent of parliamentary positions. Collectively, these countries "hold the secret to gender equality."[208]

One might be surprised to find that less than 35 percent of STEM graduates in Norway and Sweden are women. While Iceland is rated as the most gender-equal society globally, women hold 40 percent of the country's managerial positions, which is 3 percent behind the United States. Only 32 percent of managers in Finland are women. In Norway, where women lead all three parties in government, men represent nearly 85 percent of general managers in private limited companies and a whopping 92 percent of general managers in public limited companies.

How can the most egalitarian societies on earth have some of the most significant gender gaps? To find out, researchers studied one of the largest gender gaps – the gap between men and women earning college degrees in STEM. In reviewing the academic achievements and interests of men and women in 67 countries, girls scored just as strongly in scientific literacy as boys.[209] This would indicate that girls should be just as interested in and likely to enter into STEM programs – but they aren't.

The relative academic strengths of girls are different than boys. Girls may score just as well in scientific literacy as boys, but on average, a girl's strongest academic subject is reading—by contrast, a boy's strongest academic subject is science. Thus, when girls reach university and begin choosing what they would like to study, they tend to lean into their strengths and pursue careers more associated with their interests and reading aptitude. On the other hand, boys lean into their academic strengths and interests and are more likely to pursue STEM pathways.

In Scandinavian countries, where welfare states are large and robust, it is easier for women to forgo lucrative STEM careers in exchange for more family time and flexibility. This, coupled with women's relative academic strengths and interests, explains why a country like Finland can have one of the world's largest gender gaps in STEM college degrees. It also explains why, in less gender-equal countries like Algeria, the gender gap in STEM can be significantly smaller than in Scandinavia.

Algeria is a North African country where women's subjugation is written into law to such an extent that a woman's husband can revoke her chosen career path if he doesn't like it. Women have less socio-economic freedom in countries like Algeria. Women there see lucrative STEM fields as a way out of their cultural and socio-economic predicament. Rather than leaning into their primary interests, desires, and strengths when entering university, Algerian women are more likely to fall back on their secondary interests and strength in science because the STEM field affords them more socio-economic opportunity. STEM fields aren't generally what they find most exciting or fulfilling – it's what they have to do to escape poverty. The more gender-equal the country, the more likely women are to pursue careers that make them happy. Those careers are generally not the STEM careers you find in Silicon Valley.

In summary, men and women favor and express personality traits differently, with varying degrees of overlap (Lynn 1997, Weisberg 2011, Del Giudice 2012). These biologically innate characteristics are universal across cultures,

> **status, and socio-economic classes (Lippa 1997, Lippa 2008, Lynn 1997). The more egalitarian a society becomes, the higher the disparity of men's and women's choices (Lippa 2010, Bihagen and Katz-Gerro, 2000, Costa 2001, Schmitt 2008, Schmitt 2016). Rigorous scientific literature supports Damore's arguments, providing evidence that points to the fact that men and women, on average, behave differently because of innate biological and psychological variation.**

These biological and psychological variances between men and women also help us explain other gender gaps that Critical Thinkers do not discuss. For instance, boys are less likely to graduate from high school than girls. Men are less likely to enroll in college than women, and they are more likely to drop out before earning a degree. Men have a shorter life expectancy than women. Men make up an overwhelming majority of the prison system population, and while they attempt suicide less often, they are nearly four times as successful at it. If you die on the job, there is a 93 percent chance you were a man, and nearly 70 percent of people admitted to substance abuse treatment programs are men. Critical Thinkers ignore these gender gaps because they do not fit into the social constructionist narrative. If there is a patriarchy, it is doing a shitty job of favoring men.

The Gender Pay Gap

Critical Thinkers not only make radical claims about the underrepresentation of women at various companies. They also make radical claims about how much those women are paid.

During the 5th democratic primary debate in 2020, presidential hopeful Kamala Harris stated that "Women are paid 80 cents on the dollar."[210] That is to say, Harris was arguing that companies pay women 20 percent less than men for doing the same work. What could explain this?

The gender pay gap is real, but it is not a result of a patriarchal society devaluing women's work. It is the result of women making different choices than men. The gender pay gap claim stems from the oversimplified interpretation of a basic calculation. Women earn "80 cents on the dollar" when one adds the weekly median earnings of all full-time working women and divides that number by the weekly median earnings of all full-time working men. However, when one adds multiple variables in to the equation, the gender pay gap vanishes.

For instance, the original gender pay gap calculation does not consider the fact that the average man works 8.4 hours each day compared to the 7.8 hours worked each day by the average woman. It also doesn't consider the fact that more men seek jobs in higher-paying fields. A majority of aerospace and chemical engineers are men, as are a majority of surgeons, computer network architects, and software developers. Women aren't making less for equal work; men are making more for unequal work.

The gender pay gap is also found within fields dominated by women. According to the simple calculation used to determine the original gender pay gap, male nurses make 18 percent more than female nurses. That is true, but it's at least partly because male nurses choose to specialize in acute care more often than female nurses do.

Even in tightly controlled environments, where all facets of the job are equal between men and women, the gender pay gap persists. A team of researchers from Harvard, studying bus and train operators from the Massachusetts Bay Transportation Authority, found that "Even in a unionized environment where work tasks are similar, hourly wages are identical, and tenure dictates promotions, female workers earn $0.89 on the male-worker dollar (weekly earnings)."[211] In the study, researchers found women worked fewer hours, took more unpaid time off, and took less advantage of overtime opportunities. Like nursing, the different choices men and women make can explain this gap. The report concludes, "At the root of these different choices is the fact that women value time and flexibility more than men."[212]

A multi-variate analysis of the gender pay gap disproves the radical claim that women are paid less for equal work. But Critical Thinkers don't care about the truth. They care only about their interpretation of the truth when viewed through the lens of their ideological commitments. In the case of the gender pay gap, a Critical Thinker assumes discrimination is taking place because everything happens within a system of oppression. They look for discrimination where it cannot possibly exist, claim they have found it, and then demand they receive preferential treatment for being the victim of it.

Take, for example, the case of Elizabeth Rowe, principal flautist of the Boston Symphony Orchestra. In July 2018, Rowe filed a gender discrimination lawsuit against her employer, claiming she was not paid as much as her male counterparts. In seeking $200,000 in "unpaid wages," Elizabeth Rowe used Critical Thinking to claim that she had been specifically targeted because of her sex and paid less than her male counterparts for the same work. Specifically, she was upset that John Ferrillo (63), the orchestra's principal oboist, was making roughly $70,000 more per year than her. Rowe didn't care that Ferrillo had two decades of additional experience, played a more difficult instrument, and had a more senior leadership role. She was unhappy with her $286,000 salary, and she forced the Boston Symphony Orchestra into a settlement.

The Global Echo Chamber

The Implicit Association Test (IAT) was developed in 1998, aiming to "educate the public about bias and to provide a "virtual laboratory" for collecting data on the internet."[213] The test creators argued that the IAT was a tool that could measure the test takers' unconscious bias. Today, the IAT forms the backbone of Diversity, Equity, and

Inclusion regimes nationwide, a tool used to "prove" that everyone has unconscious biases against black Americans and women.

Google's "bias busting" workshops relied on the validity of the IAT to coerce employees into accepting the dictates of Critical Thinkers. Google relied on the test to label employees as sexist and racist. This is a massive problem because the IAT does not measure racism or sexism. The IAT, according to the scientists who actually created it, "does not meet the standards of measurement reliability for diagnostic use."[214] In a meta-analysis of nearly 500 students and roughly 80,000 participants, researchers discovered that "changes in implicit measures did not mediate changes in explicit measures or behavior." That is to say, even when individuals hold unconscious biases, those biases do not predict their behavior. The test is so inaccurate that one's results can vary wildly from test to test. The IAT doesn't do what people think it does.

For two decades, the Implicit Association Test has been used to justify mandatory diversity training. Businesses tell their employees that they are secretly sexist and racist, acting upon their discriminatory beliefs through microaggressions and other forms of oppression. Organizations tell employees that they unconsciously think and act in ways that subvert the power and authority of marginalized groups within their ranks. Employees believe there is nothing they can do to remedy this because it is unconscious, yet they are shamed into apologizing for it anyway by denouncing their sex, skin color, culture, or creed. If Critical Thinkers preside over a religion, then unconscious bias is their original sin.

Critical Thinkers use the IAT to ram postmodern neo-Marxist Critical Theory down the throats of employees, administrators, and officials. If everyone can be labeled a sexist or a racist at the subconscious level, then it is impossible for people like James Damore ever to take the moral high ground. No matter what the facts, logic, and evidence are, anyone who challenges the Critical Thinker can be said to be acting out their prejudicial attitudes.

Google did not fire James Damore for advancing harmful gender stereotypes. He was fired because he refused to entertain a falsehood. He was fired for defending a woman's right not to be forced to behave and act as a man does.

Why is any of this important? Why does it matter that one man was fired for saying something his employer didn't like? It matters because the truth matters. If we value truth, we must speak it to the world. We must defend the courageous individual's right to stand in opposition to tyranny and not participate in the lie.

The very foundations of liberalism – science, reason, rationality, individuality, equality of opportunity – are no longer tolerated at the points where they come into contact with the Critical Thinker's orthodoxy. Both Critical Thinkers and James Damore agree that the gender gap exists – this is undeniable – but their understanding of and strategies for addressing it are polar opposites. Critical Thinkers dictate the idea that equity must deployed to force a fix. This means that we begin preferentially treating people based on their immutable characteristics, and we don't stop doing so until everyone is guaranteed equality of outcome in representation, wealth, security, and happiness. This is an extremely illiberal approach born out of an incorrect interpretation of the data. Damore argues that we should continue to value equality of opportunity, recognizing the fact that women, on average, are different than men in their career preferences. Recognizing this doesn't mean we discriminate against women; it means we encourage women to work in technical roles and provide them with the resources they need to be successful should they want to pursue a career in computer programming – without forcing it on them. This is a liberal approach and solution that values individuality and freedom above all else.

In the last decade, Critical Thinkers have captured Google, Twitter, Facebook, Microsoft, and Apple. These companies now openly favor hiring people based on sex and skin color. They openly subscribe to an ideology that believes men and women aren't different, and that no longer draws a distinction between the sexes at all. What's worse, these companies are increasingly dictating how the rest of the world accesses information. They determine what information we can see and what information we can't see. They decide who can say what and who should be silenced. What happens when Google's ideological echo chamber targets not only employees that it deems to be sexist and racist but everyday people as well? What happens when these companies begin to discard truth in favor of Critical Thinking, forcing everyone else to play the game?

We all become James Damore.

CHAPTER NINE

REALITY DISMANTLED

"A decline in courage may be the most striking feature that an outside observer notices in the West today. The Western world has lost its civic courage, both as a whole and separately, in each country, in each government, in each political party, and of course, in the United Nations. Such a decline in courage is particularly noticeable among the ruling and intellectual elites, causing an impression of a loss of courage by the entire society."

–Aleksandr Solzhenitsyn,
A World Split Apart, Harvard
Commencement Address, 1978

If there is a lesson to be learned from the Google Memo affair, it is this – when we give Critical Thinkers positions of power, they will use that power to silence speakers of truth. James Damore had the facts on his side. His arguments were well within reason and supported by an overwhelming amount of scientific literature. But none of that mattered. Critical Thinkers burn and bury anyone or anything that forces them to deal with a reality that would challenge their postmodern playground.

When Critical Thinkers are allowed to corrupt a company as influential as Google, they begin to tear down the walls of reality. They choose what can be said and what cannot be said. It starts with adherence; everyone must jump into the canoe. Once there, Critical Thinkers coerce employees to perform sacred rituals of grievance. Employees must confess their white privilege, white fragility, and white ignorance. Brown, black, and Asian Americans must acknowledge their false consciousness. Men must apologize and atone for their toxic masculinity. These rituals drain individuals of any moral authority they might have. To suggest that anything is wrong with the way Critical Thinkers are running things highlights how bigoted, sexist, and racist one must be. To make such suggestions is to be complicit in a rotten system. Those who speak up are put on trial and ceremonially sacrificed to send a message to others; dissent will not be tolerated. Saying something as innocuous as "men are different, on average, to women" can get you fired.

James Damore wasn't advancing harmful gender stereotypes. He was defending women. By saying that men and women are different, he was arguing that it's OK for men and women to make different career choices and pursue their values and interests, whatever those might be. He was saying that we shouldn't expect men and women to be the same thing; that, if we were to follow that belief to its logical end, the dismantling of women's rights and freedoms would be the result. The truth is that men and women are different, and to subvert reality and force equal outcomes necessarily means that some women will be forced to do things they would rather not do. If anything, Google was doing the stereotyping; the company was advancing the idea that women must be expected to make the same choices and decisions as men.

When we discard truth in favor of Critical Thinking, we open Pandora's Box. If being a man or a woman means nothing – if it's all just social constructions and power dynamics – then there is no justification for protecting women's rights because the category of "women" loses any meaning that would justify such protection. Women become nothing more than pawns, moved around as necessary to occupy certain spaces when power is needed and sacrificed altogether when necessary.

Nowhere is this more evident than in the gender identity and transgender movements. Women are silenced for speaking truth to the world; women's safety is no longer paramount. This means that young girls are offered up to child abusers who would see their brains, agency, and bodies destroyed.

Gender Trouble

The terms sex and gender used to be interchangeable. Not anymore.

The idea that sex and gender are different things is a recent phenomenon. In 1949, Simone de Beauvoir wrote *The Second Sex* and inspired generations of feminists to think about sex and gender differently. Specifically, she introduced the idea that "one is not born, but rather becomes, a woman."[215]

Beauvoir claimed that psychological and behavioral differences between men and women resulted from social construction, not biology. In her view, there was a distinction between sex – the chromosomes, sex organs, hormones, and physical features one has – and gender – the social role and behaviors a person acts out into the world.

This distinction does have some truth to it. The idea that we should remove broad categorizations of what gender *must* mean is a good thing. Everyone has the agency to determine how they want to orient themselves in the world. Removing this agency and stamping everyone with the behavioral expectations of their biology is wrong. The average man and the average woman do behave in predictable ways. Biology can help us understand much of this. But to pretend that culture does not influence the behaviors of men and women is easily disproven. If the behaviors of men and women could be reduced entirely to biology, the world wouldn't have the richness of culture that it does.

Judith Butler, an American Philosopher and Critical Thinker, was inspired by Beauvoir's analysis of sex and gender. But Butler took the analysis much further, critiquing Beauvoir's ideas in a 1990 book called *Gender Trouble: Feminism and the Subversion of Identity*.

In *Gender Trouble*, Butler argues that one's gender is not rooted in a "sexed body," but instead is a performance; a rehearsal of expectations that have been socially constructed and forced on "men" and "women" to conform with the prevailing white, heterosexual, Eurocentric cultural norms of society. According to Butler, one "becomes" their gender rather than "having" a gender.

Like the Critical Thinkers who came before her, Butler's understanding of the world is one of subjectivity and power hierarchies, a universe of social construction where language and discourse are used to marginalize, police, and punish anyone who does not conform to normal expectations. In Butler's view, this system has produced the male/female binary as a way of privileging certain values, beliefs, and behaviors over others.

Butler theorized that biological sex itself was a social construct that, without understanding gender in the traditional sense, as sex=gender and gender=sex, becomes unintelligible. Butler writes, "If the immutable character of sex is contested, perhaps this construct called 'sex' is as culturally constructed as gender; indeed, perhaps it was always already gender, with the consequence that the distinction between sex and gender turns out to be no distinction at all.[216] Understanding Butler's arguments – that sex and gender are socially constructed, one and the same – is essential to understanding the gender identity and transgender movements of today.

Butler argues that masculinity and femininity do not precede a physical sexed body. She suggests that "the body becomes its gender through a series of acts which are renewed, revised, and consolidated through time." One, in her view, does not "have" masculine or feminine psychologies, behaviors, or attributes; one is born as a blank slate waiting to be stamped by the world. This stamping process is done by asserting that individuals need to ritualistically perform specific actions to establish hierarchies and normalcy. Gender distinctions, in Butler's view, were established as a "strategy of survival," which "is a performance with clearly punitive consequences."[217] For Butler, the gender dynamic has been socially constructed to situate everyone neatly within heteronormative cultures. It is a means of control. By constructing this binary dynamic and demanding people perform in accordance with it, society can punish those who are "performing their gender wrong." It can also celebrate someone for performing it well.

Butler's theory of "gender performativity" attempts to arrest power back from the system of gender oppression that she defines. In her view, a "woman" is nothing more than a socially constructed set of norms forced on "sexed bodies." To break this violent oppression, Butler suggests that people ridicule the gender norms of society by performing in drag and cross-dressing; she encourages people to "perform," repeatedly, a gender other than their own. Through this repeated performance, one actively resists society's norms; one "becomes" the gender they express. In other words, the categories of sex and gender are purposefully made unstable; they are dismantled.

Today, Judith Butler is the Maxine Elliot Professor in the Department of Comparative Literature and the Program of Critical Theory at the University of California, Berkley. Since its inception, Butler's radical theory of gender performativity has taken college campuses, corporate America, and the world by storm. For the political left, Butler's Queer Theory (a critical theory of gender) provides a framework for understanding the issues that James Damore highlighted in his Google Memo. It asserts that privileged white, heterosexual, Western men cause and propagate the gender gap in tech. Women are marginalized, policed, and punished for performing their gender differently than the straight, white, male-dominated hierarchy allows. Women are less represented and make less money than men not because of individual sexists, differing biological or psychological characteristics, or choice, but because the system itself fights to uphold its dominant values in phantom, yet ever-present ways.

Judith Butler's work heavily inspired the gender identity and transgender movements of the last three decades. In deconstructing biological sex and gender, adherents of Butler's Queer Theory were inspired to identify primarily with their feelings rather than any concrete biological category. It didn't matter if a person had a penis – they could now literally "become" a woman because the category "woman" had been stripped of all meaning. It didn't matter if a person had a uterus – they could now literally "become" a man for the same reason. People were free to "be" whatever it was they said they wanted to be.

Silencing Women

By adhering to the works of Queer Theorists like Judith Butler, Critical Thinkers have created a gender identity craze among children and teenagers. Critical Thinkers feed young boys and girls a critical theory of gender that destabilizes their perceptions of who they are and how they might orient themselves in the world.

Critical Thinkers teach kids that, rather than being a boy or a girl, a "he" or a "she," they can identify as a "zir," "them," "emself," "demon," or "xem." There are over 100 gender pronouns that children are encouraged to use based on how they would like to identify and perform their gender. These kids learn about Queer Theory in school (through Critical Pedagogy) and on social media platforms like TikTok, Tumblr, Facebook, and Twitter. These messages are amplified on popular television series and in mainstream medical institutions.

Critical Thinkers also teach children that society must affirm their gender. To not do so is considered a violent act. If a child decides they identify as and prefer to be called a xenomorph, then addressing that child as anything else is to commit a hate crime. The consequences for "misgendering" can be devastating; a father in Canada was recently jailed for addressing his 14-year-old, gender non-conforming, transgender identifying biologically female child as "daughter," "she," and "her."[218]

Many children are now being taught that they can literally become members of the opposite sex. If a girl likes to play with boys' toys or rough house, Critical Thinkers will tell that girl that she can transition and "become" a boy if that gender identity makes her feel better. If a boy likes to wear dresses or paint his fingernails, Critical Thinkers will tell him that he can transition and "become" a girl for the same reasons.

All people feel uncomfortable in their bodies at some point in their lives. Young girls are especially susceptible to negative feelings about their outward appearance. But the depression, anxiety, and confusion that was once considered a normal part of adolescent puberty – something that, for most people, fades in time – is now being weaponized by Critical Thinkers to manufacture a gender crisis in teenagers. An increasing number of these kids are being told they should do irreversible damage to their bodies to "become" whatever they want to be. And no one is stopping them.

Between 2016 and 2017, the number of girls and women seeking gender confirmation surgeries in the United States quadrupled. [219] Critical Thinkers have convinced thousands of teenagers that they should change their outward appearance to match whatever they "feel" on the inside. These children are taught that transitioning into the gender of their choice is the only thing that will ease their suffering.

In 2020, investigative journalist Abigail Shrier wrote *Irreversible Damage: The Transgender Craze Seducing Our Daughters* to call attention to the "severe spike in transgender identification among adolescent girls"[220] What Shrier discovered was shocking:

"Thousands of teen girls across the Western world are not only self-diagnosing with a real dysphoric condition they likely do not have; in many cases, they are obtaining hormones and surgeries following the most cursory diagnostic processes. Schoolteachers, therapists, doctors, surgeons, and medical-accreditation organizations are all rubber-stamping these transitions, often out of fear that doing otherwise will be reported as a sign of 'transphobia' – despite growing evidence that most young people who present as trans will eventually desist, and so these interventions will do more harm than good."[221]

Before 2012, researchers thought gender dysphoria – a mental condition "characterized by a severe and persistent discomfort in one's biological sex" – only afflicted 0.01 percent of the population. What was once an incredibly rare diagnosis, one which overwhelmingly afflicted men, was now being diagnosed primarily in increasing numbers of young girls. In the UK, for instance, the number of young girls reporting that they are experiencing gender dysphoria in recent years is up 4,400 percent over the previous decade.

Critical Thinkers attribute the rising rates of trans-identifying children to a broader societal acceptance of transgender people. They argue that what they are doing is working. They are tearing down systems of oppression and allowing kids to "be" who they really are. Shrier challenged this narrative, arguing that the very same groups of teenage girls that have historically struggled with anxiety, cutting, and anorexia were suffering from a new peer contagion; transgenderism. These girls were not coming out as transgender because they had gender dysphoria; they were identifying as transgender because they had been fed an ideology that promises to make them whole. These girls are going through a challenging stage of life that nearly all women face. Critical Thinkers have convinced them that if they feel at all uncomfortable in their skin, they can shed it for a new one.

They can become something radically different and eliminate their suffering in the process.

Abigail Shrier wrote her book as a woman concerned about young women's mental and physical health. She had conducted hundreds of interviews with transgender individuals, many of whom regretted their decisions to transition early in life. Shrier specifically stated that she was not against transitioning altogether. In her view, we should leave the enormity of that decision to adults, not children. The consequences of gender-affirming therapy and treatment can lead to infertility later in life. What child is capable of making that decision?

For her efforts, Shrier was labeled a bigot, transphobe, and TERF (trans-exclusionary radical feminist) by Critical Thinkers for daring to challenge an ideology that celebrates prescribing hormone blockers to children as young as 10, and for questioning whether or not it's a good idea to allow 13-year-old girls to receive testosterone and double mastectomies after a self-diagnosis of gender dysphoria. For this, Shrier would be dragged through the mud and held up as a warning sign to others.

On Twitter, one lawyer from the American Civil Liberties Union (ACLU) tweeted, "Stopping the circulation of this book and these ideas is 100% a hill I will die on."

The American Booksellers Association (APA) apologized for sending booksellers copies of *Irreversible Damage* in its bi-monthly "white box," which generally includes new titles that sellers may be interested in ordering. The APA took to Twitter to write, "This is a serious, violent incident that goes against ABA's ends policies, values, and everything we believe and support. It is inexcusable."[222]

After appearing on *The Joe Rogan Experience* to discuss her investigation, Spotify employees demanded that Shrier's discussion with the most prominent podcaster on the planet be removed from the platform. Employees at Target and Amazon made similar attempts to ban Shrier's book from the marketplace.

It's tempting to say that Abigail Shrier was "canceled" following the publication of her whistleblower's report. But that's not what happened. Shrier's *challenge* to gender ideology was canceled. Critical Thinkers will not allow dissenting ideas to emerge and threaten their narrative control. As Shrier described in an article explaining the efforts to silence her, "The controversy delivered a warning shot to other media companies: Unless you want trouble, do not challenge the narrative of unquestioning "affirmation" for every child who claims to be trans – no matter the age, context, or lack of responsible medical oversight provided to the family."[223]

Critical Thinkers have canceled other prominent critics of the gender identity and trans movement for their courage. In 2018, a researcher for a non-profit global think tank – Maya Forstater – criticized proposed reforms to the United Kingdom's Gender Recognition Act of 2004 that would allow people to self-identify as whatever gender or sex they chose. On Twitter, Forstater wrote;

"Everyone's equality and safety should be protected, but women and girls lose out on privacy, safety and fairness if males are allowed into changing rooms, dormitories, prisons, sports teams."

For making such views public, Forstater lost a chance to renew her contract with the Centre for Global Development. She was accused of "offensive and exclusionary" language by a Central London employment tribunal and found guilty. In speaking to the ruling, Forstater tweeted, "My belief... is that sex is a biological fact, and is immutable. There are two sexes, male and female. Men and boys are male. Women and girls are female. It is impossible to change sex. These were until very recently understood as basic facts of life by almost everyone."[224]

J.K. Rowling, one of the most successful authors to have ever lived, was canceled by a voracious twitter mob for coming to Forstater's defense.

"Dress however you please. Call yourself whatever you like. Sleep with any consenting adult who'll have you. Live your best life in peace and security. But force women out of their jobs for stating that sex is real? #IStandWithMaya #This IsNotADrill"

The message is clear. It's OK to harass and silence women if it suits an ideological purpose. To be specific, if any woman speaks out against the erasure of women's identity, they are to be tarred, feathered, and removed from the public square.

Erasing Women

Critical Thinkers have destabilized gender and sex-based categories. As a result, women's spaces are increasingly occupied by those who have not been born women; they are occupied by those who have become women.

Consider the movement to include biological males in female sports. Critical Thinkers argue that there is no distinction between someone born a woman and someone who says they are a woman. Therefore, if a biological male decides that he is a woman, he should compete with other women in sporting events. Not allowing him to do so is to deny *her* the dignity *she* deserves.

Fallon Fox, a transwoman (biological male), fought two professionally sanctioned mixed martial arts bouts before acknowledging that she had been born a man in an interview. Fox slammed her opponent in her first professional bout, dislocating Elisha Helsper's arm before finishing the fight with elbows to the head. In her second fight, Fox knocked Ericka Newsome unconscious with a vicious knee to the skull. Neither of her first two opponents knew they were fighting a biological male who had undergone gender reassignment surgery[225].

Fox didn't lose her mixed martial arts license after revealing that she had been born a man. Commissioners allowed her to continue fighting women because of her extensive hormone therapy treatment. Critical Thinkers argued that because Fox's testosterone levels were now within the legal range for the women's division she was fighting in, stripping her of her license would be transphobic. It cannot be said too often that, under Critical Orthodoxy, a human being is the sex they tell you they are. What is typically considered "biological sex" is nothing more than a subjective assignment determined at birth by someone with an agenda.

Even though Fox had undergone extensive treatment to affirm her gender, it doesn't change the fact that the underlying biological mechanisms that govern her body are biologically male. She lived as a man for three decades. No amount of hormonal treatment can change the fact that she had a distinct physical advantage over any biological female she competed with.

On average, men have larger frames – bigger and longer bones – that give them a distinct mechanical advantage over women. They also have stronger ligaments, faster reaction times, and greater lung capacity. These advantages translate into a deadly difference between the two sexes and their abilities to inflict physical punishment on other human beings. Whether by hand, elbow, shin, or knee, Fallon Fox was unquestionably more suited to do battle than her biologically female opponents. One of these opponents, Tamikka Brents, who lost to Fox via technical knockout in 2014, described the shocking amount of strength she encountered when fighting Fox in the cage.

"I've fought a lot of women and have never felt the strength that I felt in a fight as I did that night. I can't answer whether it's because she was born a man or not because I'm not a doctor. I can only say, I've never felt so overpowered ever in my life and I am an abnormally strong female in my own right. Her grip was different. I could usually move around in the clinch against other females but couldn't move at all in Fox's clinch."[226]

Setting a precedent for allowing biological men to fight biological women in a cage illustrates just how far Critical Thinkers are willing to go to adhere to their ideology. There is no sport in which the consequences of placing a man versus a woman could be more brutal than mixed martial arts. The delusion of Critical Thinkers has no limits; they expect biological women to enthusiastically suit up for a chance to have their skull fractured by a biological male to ally themselves with "progress."

Although they are not being physically beaten with punches and kicks, girls and women across the country are increasingly expected to compete with biological boys and men.

In 2017, 2018, and 2019 the Connecticut State Championships for girls track was dominated by transgender girls. In 2017, Andraya Yearwood won the 100-meter and 200-meter dash. In 2018 and 2019, Terry Miller would win both titles, along with a girl's state record in the 55-meter event.

In 2020, the University of Montana's Jonathan Eastwood ran the women's mile 4.5 seconds faster than the next best competitor at the Big Sky Conference indoor championships. Eastwood, a transgender woman with a year of hormone therapy under her belt, had placed 7th in the men's 1,500-meter event the year before.

In 2019, Franklin Pierce University's (FPU) CeCe Telfer won the NCAA Women's Division II Outdoor Track and Field Championship's 400-meter hurdles event. The official Twitter account of FPU celebrated Telfer's win with a tweet;

"In just its 7th year of existence, the @FPURavensXCTF has its first national champion. Senior CeCe Telfer took control of the 400-meter hurdles on Sat. PM and went on to post victory w/ a personal best time of 57.53."

In 2021, University of Pennsylvania swimmer Lia Thomas broke records in the 500-yard and 200-yard freestyle events at the Zippy Invitational in Akron, Ohio. In The 1,650 freestyle, she won by more than 38 seconds.[227] Lurking somewhere in the absurdity of this dominant performance are the dreams of women that will never be as fast as Thomas, no matter what commitment, determination, or innate talents and abilities they may possess.

Whether in the cage, on the track, or in a swimming pool, biological women are being gaslighted into thinking that biological woman have the same physical capabilities as biological men. Critical Thinkers coerce athletic commissions into thinking that a man with artificially lowered testosterone levels has no vestigial advantages over the woman he is competing with. This is why, in the NCAA, a biological man need only take testosterone suppression treatment for a single year before becoming eligible to compete in women's divisions.

The fastest women in the world cannot compete with high school boys. For example, boys between the ages of 14 and 18 have faster world record times in 21 of 22 track and field events when compared to adult women. By 14, boys are setting faster times in the 200m, 400m, 800m, 1500m, high jump, hammer throw, and javelin events. The only event in which the fastest women in the world best high school boys is the marathon. Young women cannot be expected to compete with biological males who are, on average, bigger, stronger, and faster than they can possibly be.

It's All About Equality

Critical Thinkers frequently use language to obfuscate their true intentions. H.R.5, better known as The Equality Act, is a shining example of how Critical Thinkers package their ideology in progressive and "inclusive" language to trick people into supporting legislation that discriminates against women.

Having passed in the U.S. House of Representatives in March of 2021, The Equality Act seeks "to prohibit discrimination on the basis of sex, gender identity, and sexual orientation, and for other purposes."[228] But we are all already protected from acts of discrimination under The Civil Rights Act of 1964. The purpose of The Equality Act isn't to prohibit discrimination. The objective is to infuse current protections with Queer Theory; to make postmodern neo-Marxist Theory law.

During a Senate Judiciary Committee hearing on The Equality Act in early 2021, Abigail Shrier testified that passing The Equality Act would erode women's rights.

"By enshrining gender identity as a protected category, this bill would make it impossible ever to legally distinguish between a woman and a biological male who claims a female identity, for whatever amount of time and for whatever reason or purpose."[229]

Proponents of the Equality Act argue that it will "finally provide consistent, explicit non-discrimination protections for LGBTQ+ people."[230] These proponents fail to mention that, as Abigail Shrier testified, doing so would make discrimination against women legal. One needn't look far to understand the implications of such a law.

In 2021, Krystal Gonzalez, a biological woman, sued the California Department of Corrections and Rehabilitation. Gonzalez alleged that she was raped by a biological man who had been transferred from a men's facility to the Central California Women's Facility after identifying as a woman. According to the suit, Gonzalez asked to be housed away from male prisoners after the alleged incident but was told that her attacker was a "transgender woman with a penis."[231] As they identified as such, California's new Transgender Respect, Agency, and Dignity Act protected Gonzalez's attacker. This "transgender woman with a penis" was one of 295 biological males that asked to be moved to women's facilities after Governor Gavin Newsom signed the bill into law in September 2020.[232]

Women in Washington and Illinois have also sued their correctional facilities after alleging that transgender women raped them. If Congress signs The Equality Act into law, any biological man who wishes to identify as a woman and transfer to a woman's facility will have the constitutionally protected right to do so.

And biological male prisoners won't be the only ones taking advantage of their new constitutionally protected "equality." Lawmakers will require us all to affirm biologically male teachers, coaches, and doctors that identify as women at whatever point in time and for whichever reasons or purposes. Young girls will be forced to share bathrooms with adult biological males, and teenage girls will be forced to share a locker room and compete with biological men.

Women will lose their rights to fairness, dignity, and privacy because Critical Thinkers have made their ideology law.

The overwhelming number of transgender men and women are good and moral people, and they do not want to trample on the rights of women. But, as with all things, Critical Thinkers have corrupted the transgender category, using it as a tool to amplify their power and force everyone to play in their fantasy world. In this respect, Critical Thinkers are actually dismantling the wishes of people who genuinely feel like they were born in the wrong bodies, and who want nothing more than to be accepted as members of the opposite sex.

These transgender men and women don't obfuscate language. They know their biology will forever mark them with characteristics, advantages, and disadvantages that cannot be changed. They understand that they are not "really" a woman; they are trans women. They know that they are not "really" a man; they are trans men. They do not want society to bend to their will. Instead, they want to fit into society. This is an intolerable position for Critical Thinkers because they think no one should fit into society as it is. To tell a young person "it gets better" is to attempt to condition that child to tolerate the evils of the current order. Critical Thinkers would rather keep kids confused, using them as an instrument of intersectional power dynamics as the walls of reality collapse around us.

In her Senate Judiciary Committee hearing, Abigail Shrier summoned the courage to fight back against the advancement of gender ideologues attempting to erase women. Shrier understands that there will always be terrible actors that take advantage of such legislative actions. She knows there are perverts, sexual predators, and violent male criminals that would love an opportunity to invade women's spaces in the name of equality. Shrier also knows that, just as everyone else has the right to life, liberty, and happiness, so too do women.

"Gender ideology, which is at the heart of this bill, is misogyny in progressive clothing. Gender ideology tells women and girls that they are not entitled to their fear or their sense of unfairness as their protective spaces are eliminated. They must never object that sports is and has always been a matter of biology, not identity. They mustn't assert that we keep women's protective spaces for biological women to ensure their physical safety regardless of how they identify."[233]

Critical Thinkers know that the number of people born intersex is fantastically small. They also know that many people who feel that they were "born in the wrong body" eventually conclude that a large part of those feelings arise from struggles with mental health. Critical Thinkers capitalize on the vulnerability of such people, using them to advance radical agendas to dismantle Western civilization. They understand that driving "mental sickness" into society, as dictated by Herbert Marcuse in the 1960s, is a viable strategy to achieve such ends.

Women like Abigail Shrier speak the truth in the face of tyranny. They do exist, and we should be careful not to erase them.

CHAPTER TEN

The Future Is Evergreen

> "I understand, I sense that you're tired. But you have not yet really suffered the terrible trials of the 20th century which have rained down on the old continent... You're tired, but the Communists who want to destroy your system are not; they're not tired at all."
>
> –Aleksandr Solzhenitsyn

Critical Thinkers are breaking America. They swing their pickaxes and hammers relentlessly, chipping away at the foundations of a liberal tradition that has brought more prosperity to the world in the last three centuries than any other organizing principle that ever existed. They do not know what lies on the other side of the rubble, but they are convinced that they must be the ones to lead us to it. With unshakeable moral conviction, they will justify any action they must take to poison and overthrow everything to bring about their revolution.

In the previous ten years, Critical Thinkers have assumed incredible institutional power; through this, they have forced us all to play inside their fantasy. We now occupy a world where racism is no longer an act of individual prejudice against another person. Racism is now a permanent, inescapable force that permeates every second of our lives. This fantasy requires us to eternally commit to tearing down societal structures to build a new, antiracist order. Those who can decipher the phantom forces of white supremacy lead the new regime, commanding from on high that everyone else must give them the power to force us all onto the warpath. Critical Thinkers consider individualism, objectivity, equality of opportunity, reason, rationality, and equal protection under the law as barriers on the battlefield. They do not tolerate debate or open inquiry; they only understand the need to disrupt and dismantle. Everything is crushed under the weight of Critical Social Justice to make way for the emergence of a new stage of history.

If the last decade seems like it doesn't make sense, that's because it doesn't. Critical Thinkers have poisoned our language, making it nearly impossible to discern between reality and postmodern fantasy. Equity is now used interchangeably with equality, although the concepts are irreconcilable. Diversity is now a mechanism for filtering those who demonstrate strict adherence to the new religious code from those who don't. Inclusive spaces are ones that are intolerant to new ideas, discourse, debate, and truth-seeking. Critical Thinkers have dismantled our very ways of communicating with one another, hollowing out words with Jacques Derrida's "deconstruction" to stuff them with new meaning to usurp power. This tactic confuses good people with decent morals, priming their minds to accept a poison that will destroy not only themselves but the ones they love. In short order, those who once espoused the greatness of liberalism are proposing to defund the police, program children, and erase women.

When students protested outside his classroom in May of 2017, Bret Weinstein said that "history could pivot on this hallway right now."[234] He could not have been more right. The Woke Warpath began long ago, but 2017 marked the definitive year Critical Orthodoxy became mainstream. Critical Thinkers had spent nearly 100 years marching through Western institutions and had finally manufactured the cultural hegemony they longed for. It was now OK to be openly racist towards white people and openly sexist towards heterosexual people; OK to call black Americans Uncle Toms for shrugging off the conspiratorial claims of their compatriots; OK to tear down statues of those who saw to it that we would become the most privileged group of people to have ever been born – Americans.

Critical Thinkers will dismantle everything – that is their only purpose. Our streets are now less safe, our children's classrooms are political factories, and the truth no longer matters. For as bad as things already are, things can and will get much worse if we don't recognize what is happening for what it really is.

The University

Critical Thinkers captured the universities decades ago. Today, the U.S. university system functions less as a vital cog in the liberal machine and more as a Critical Social Justice assembly line. It is not uncommon to find campuses saturated with diversity bureaucrats, all of whom are charged with coercing faculty, administrators, and children into developing a critical consciousness. The Ohio State pays 132 diversicrats enough to offset the tuition of roughly 1,100 students. If students can't pick up enough grievance, discontent, and victimhood from this cohort of Critical Thinkers, they certainly can from their professors. Across the U.S., 1 in 5 social scientists openly identifies as Marxist.

The social sciences bred the various postmodern and critical theories that now plague engineering, math, psychics, and chemistry departments. Empiricism and objectivity couldn't save these fields, for Critical Thinkers have dismantled the Enlightenment toolkit. Lawrence Krauss, a world-renowned physicist and outspoken critic of superstitious truth claims, is one of many thousand scientists in the U.S who has warned about the corruption of his field.

"Academic science leaders have adopted wholesale the language of dominance and oppression previously restricted to 'cultural studies' journals to guide their disciplines, to censor dissenting views, to remove faculty from leadership positions if their research is claimed by opponents to support systemic oppression."

Every top-tier STEM university in the United States has abandoned its mission as a purveyor of truth. The California Institute of Technology (Caltech), Stanford, Carnegie Mellon, and the Georgia Institute for Technology (Georgia Tech) are now less concerned with merit, equality, and fairness and more concerned with making hiring decisions based on skin color and sex.

MIT administrators canceled Dorian Abbot's guest lecture in late 2021 because he dared to critique the DEI regimes on college campuses that would make identity Marxists of us all. Abbot, a prominent geophysicist at the University of Chicago, had written an article critical of affirmative action, writing:

"DEI violates the ethical and legal principle of equal treatment. It entails treating people as members of a group rather than as individuals, repeating the mistake that made possible the atrocities of the 20th century. It requires being willing to tell an applicant 'I will ignore your merits and qualifications and deny you admission because you belong to the wrong group, and I have defined a more important social objective that justifies doing so.' It treats persons as merely means to an end, giving primacy to a statistic over the individuality of a human being."[235]

Every elite university in the country now celebrates hiring decisions based on skin color and sex. Physics, chemistry, engineering, and mathematics departments proudly monitor candidates for the level of melanin in their skin and the plumbing between their legs. With equity statements in hand, administrators openly discriminate against qualified candidates in the process of redistributing privilege and power. This is, of course, extremely racist and sexist.

By sacrificing excellence, equality, and fairness at the altar of Critical Social Justice, campus administrators are dooming America's ability to remain the world leader in science and technology. While Critical Thinkers are condemning math for being racist and chemistry for being "too white," China is testing hypersonic missiles that have "stunned" General John Hyten, former vice chairman of the Joint Chiefs of Staff. These missiles could one day allow China to launch a surprise nuclear attack on the U.S.

Critical Thinkers have used their postmodern neo-Marxist Critical theories to corrupt the very idea that the scientific process is a legitimate pathway to knowledge. They have done this before in Nazi Germany and the Soviet Union, where "Jewish" and "Western" science were assumed to be contaminated by the worldviews of their practitioners. Millions starved to death as a result.

Healthcare

Consider a future where healthcare providers are race-conscious, offering treatments based on skin color. In *Is It Lawful and Ethical to Prioritize Racial Minorities for COVID-19 Vaccines?*, authors from Harvard, Georgetown, and the University of Pennsylvania write:

"The National Academies of Sciences, Engineering, and Medicine (NASEM) has recommended prioritization of racial minorities who are 'worse off" socioeconomically and epidemiologically. The World Health Organization (WHO) similarly cautioned that 'colorblind' allocation frameworks could perpetuate or exacerbate existing injustices. Both NASEM and WHO urge policy makers to allocate vaccines in ways that reduce unjust health disparities."[236]

Critical Thinkers have captured the NASEM and WHO and are now using their power to apply Critical Race Theory to medicine. Rather than allocating vaccines to color-blind categories based on the most vulnerable populations – the elderly – these institutions argue that we should instead view the world through the lens of race communism and vaccinate specific socially constructed identity categories first. This proposal would have been considered overtly racist ten years ago but is now commonplace. Utah, Vermont, and Montana gave priority vaccine access to "Black adults and people from other minority communities" in early 2021.[237] Many other states allocated various percentages of their overall vaccine allotments to people based on skin color. Massachusetts, New Hampshire, North Carolina, and Connecticut set aside doses for "historically marginalized populations"[238] rather than targeting all people with preexisting conditions and comorbidities. California reserved a whopping 40 percent for "underserved communities."[239] Critical Thinkers in these states did all of this in the name of health equity.

Like all forms of equity, "health equity" is a morally bankrupt concept. Those who advocate for it have developed a critical consciousness, believing that all health disparities result from socially imposed forces on powerless peoples. People aren't fat because they eat too much and exercise too little; they are fat because of capitalism, sexism, and racism. They have no control over their eating because they don't control the means of their food production, have no access to proper nutrition, and are victimized by greedy, racist food manufacturers – or so the Critical Thinkers will tell you.

Mayo Clinic, the number one ranked hospital in the United States, has adopted a health equity mission. The website for the Center for Health Equity and Community Engagement at Mayo states that:

"Racism is a key determinant of health and is pervasive and deeply embedded in society and the practices of institutions that train the health care workforce... initiatives that meaningfully address racism will benefit everyone, but require dismantling embedded structural racism throughout the pathway from cradle to career... institutions should strategically realign their missions, visions and values to enable reconciliation on racism, psychological safety for Black people, racial diversity, racial inclusivity and health justice."[240]

In other words, Mayo Clinic has now committed to health communism (justice and communism are synonymous in Critical Social Justice Theory). There can be no more complex explanation than racism for health disparities, which means Mayo will use equity to redistribute power and resources until our healthcare system is controlled entirely by postmodern neo-Marxists.

The Critical Thinkers at Mayo are joined by others across the country in properly dismantling much of our healthcare systems. It is not uncommon for healthcare providers to give expecting mothers brochures for "chestfeeding." Breastfeeding would imply that all women have breasts, to the exclusion of transwomen. It is also not uncommon for teen girls to receive healthcare tips for "vulva owners" or "menstruators." Critical Thinkers consider trans women (or any other person who says they identify as such at any point in time) to be women. Therefore, regardless of their biologically male plumbing, we must all believe they too "own vulvas" and bleed. If Critical Thinkers are allowed to see the process of disrupting and dismantling through to its logical end, the category of "woman" will cease to exist. If those who practice medicine treat biologically male and female bodies the same people will die. That is unquestionable.

Antiracist Constitution

Critical Thinkers are actively attempting to make their worldview law. Ibram X. Kendi advocates for the passage of an antiracist constitutional amendment that would quite literally make the United States the world's first country governed by race communists. Here is Kendi's proposal in full;

"To fix the original sin of racism, Americans should pass an antiracist amendment to the U.S. Constitution that enshrines two guiding antiracist principals [sic]: Racial inequity is evidence of racist policy and the different racial groups are equals. The amendment would make unconstitutional racial inequity over a certain threshold, as well as racist ideas by public officials (with 'racist ideas' and 'public official' clearly defined). It would establish and permanently fund the Department of Anti-racism (DOA) comprised of formally trained experts on racism and no political appointees. The DOA would be responsible for preclearing all local, state and federal public policies to ensure they won't yield racial inequity, monitor those policies, investigate private racist policies when racial inequity surfaces, and monitor public officials for expressions of racist ideas. The DOA would be empowered with disciplinary tools to wield over and against policymakers and public officials who do not voluntarily change their racist policy and ideas."[241]

The idea that all racial inequality is "evidence of racist policy" is insane and can't be believed by a thinking person. If we allow people who think in this way to govern the world, it will lead to the institution of actual racism, not the fantasy version by which Kendi and others consider themselves to be victimized.

To illustrate just how quickly this proposed antiracist amendment would turn disastrous, consider this – Indian Americans have a median household income of $126,000, and Taiwanese and Filipino Americans aren't that far behind. Of the 16 most populous Asian American groups in the U.S., including people from Vietnam, Pakistan, China, and Indonesia, only one group has a lower median household income than "white" Americans. According to Kendi's proposed amendment, there is something racist going on here that Critical Thinkers must dismantle to redistribute wealth and force equal outcomes. And the Kendilytes wouldn't stop with Asian Americans; they would also tackle the supposed racist policies that see Nigerian, Polynesian, Ecuadorian, Ghanaian, and Portuguese Americans situated above "white" Americans at the top of U.S. median household income charts. By what means would we achieve justice in this scenario? Would Kendi propose to limit the income of these "historically marginalized" ethnic groups? Would he see these people less represented in lucrative careers? Would he limit the number of business licenses afforded to foreigners taking the ultimate risk of starting a business in America? Would he forcibly remove these people and situate others in their place? The communists never tell.

And what's this nonsense about asking us all to trust a small group of individuals to become the sole arbiters of truth, determining what is and what is not to be considered a racist idea? Kendi quite literally is advocating not for a Department of Antiracism, but a *Dictatorship of Antiracists*. Is this group to consist of the students that rioted for justice at Evergreen in 2017? Perhaps we can draw from the ranks of those grooming children in schools or advocating for the dissolution of America's police forces. According to Kendi, racist ideas include merit, standardized testing, and equal opportunity. Will his antiracist methods help America rid herself of such cancer?

By "formally trained experts on racism," Kendi means "Critical Race Theorists." These modern-day race commissars would be in charge of governing us all with fantastically illiberal laws and properly psychopathic intentions. If implemented, there wouldn't be enough space in the gulag for everyone who had once thought the insanity would stop at their doorstep. In short, Kendi and his supporters would create a department of unelected officials with the power to dismantle America in its entirety. Rather than relying on cultural hegemony, this cabal of Critical Thinkers would rewrite our nation's laws to achieve communism without the consent of the governed. Americans have spent the last 400 years gradually taking social significance out of racial categories. Kendi would see to it that we put it back in.

The Fight For Social Justice

The human desire to be free catalyzed the social justice movement that saw Civil Rights leaders march on Washington to demand constitutionally protected equal rights. Dr. Martin Luther King Jr. was joined by those who insisted that America make good on the promissory note that was the Declaration of Independence. These leaders did not demand that the government force everyone to be equal. Instead, they demanded the inalienable right to pursue the very things that make us all unequal. They demanded that their countrymen and women see them for what they were – Americans.

Critical Thinkers despise the irreducible complexity of the individual. They do everything in their power to make every American believe that they belong to intersecting groups and that those categorizations mean something. The question is why? Why do Critical Thinkers place such social significance on identity categories? Why do they believe that your immutable characteristics determine what you believe and how you should view the world? Why are they so damn set on forcing us all to be equal along every conceivable dimension?

In an interview in 1969, Max Horkheimer, the father of Critical Theory, laid bare the answer to these questions.

"Marx did not see that freedom and justice are dialectical concepts. The more freedom, the less justice and the more justice, the less freedom."[242]

Critical Thinkers believe that freedom and justice contradict one another. To achieve their justice, they must limit the unalienable freedoms we enjoy as Americans. Justice, in their eyes, is some inconceivable future place and time where all peoples share in the joy of cookie-cutter lives in which every person is forced into equal life outcomes. The freedom to choose what you're interested in, where you focus your energy, what you study, what you do for work, how you raise a family, and how you live your life are choices Critical Thinkers cannot tolerate. If people are free to make different decisions and embody the diversity of the human spirit, then there will never be a world in which we are all equal.

Critical Thinkers place social significance on identity categories because the revolution would not be possible without group agitation and accelerated tribalism. They need people to feel that power and privilege are organizing the world along a continuum of oppression. Critical Thinkers create radical divisions along the lines of class, race, sex, and ability. They sow discontent, victimhood, mental illness, and anxiety to energize a revolutionary force that would tear down America and force the latest iteration of communism on us all.

Critical Thinkers also believe the outcomes of our lives are structurally determined because that is precisely how they wish it to be. The fact that freedom allows people to be different and express their life in whichever way they choose is antithetical to the Critical Thinkers' goal of justice. They seek the power to redistribute privilege, access, resources, opportunity, and wealth to force us all into the utopian vision of communism that they believe to be the final stage of history. Although the means and modes of revolution have changed, we must never forget that these people are Marxists to the bone. They hate freedom because their worldview does not accommodate difference.

Critical Thinkers practice Critical Social Justice to disrupt and dismantle everything on the warpath to revolution. The insanity must stop. The only form of social justice that matters is one rooted in individualism. If we lose that, then we lose everything.

The Woke Warpath has consumed nearly every institution in America, but hope has not yet been lost. Millions of people in this country still value liberalism on both the right and the left sides of the political aisle. Some of these courageous anti-woke warriors are not only pushing back against the Critical Orthodoxy we find in our schools and workplaces, but they are winning critical battles.

Critical Battles

There are two critical battles that defenders of liberalism must win to combat the Woke Warpath in our communities, workplaces, schools, and government. The first is to understand what Critical Thinkers believe. It behooves free thinkers to learn the history of the postmodern neo-Marxist philosophical tradition – to learn why Critical Thinkers think and act the way they do and how their worldview stands in direct contradiction to American values.

This book does explore a rudimentary history of Critical Thinking. But its true purpose was to demonstrate that contemporary movements for social justice are little more than attempts to break society to spark a Marxian revolution. That is to say, the purpose of this book is to demonstrate that Critical Thinkers are breaking America and to argue that this catastrophic problem must be addressed immediately.

To delve further into the Critical Mind, one must study the philosophical battle that has enveloped the modern world for the last four centuries. *Explaining Postmodernism: Skepticism and Socialism from Rousseau to Foucault* by Stephen R. C. Hicks is an excellent means to achieve this end. In his book, Hicks takes his readers on a fantastic journey, tracing the philosophical roots of liberalism, Critical Theory, and postmodernism back to the Enlightenment and Counter-Enlightenment. These philosophies underpin our constitutional republic and the identity communism that wishes to usurp it. It's essential to understand the basic history of each to wrap one's head around the roots of the Woke Warpath and the attacks Critical Thinkers level against liberal democracy.

With the big picture under your belt, consider picking up a copy of *Cynical Theories: How Activist Scholarship Made Everything About Race, Gender, and Identity—and Why This Harms Everybody* by Helen Pluckrose and James Lindsay. In their book, Pluckrose and Lindsay focus on the development and spread of postmodern and neo-Marxist critical theories in the universities. Pluckrose and Lindsay do an excellent job describing how activists and scholars have infected our institutions of knowledge production with postmodern neo-Marxism. For thousands of readers worldwide, these authors were among the first to properly identify the illiberal rot that underpins much of the academic machine.

Both *Explaining Postmodernism* and *Cynical Theories* help readers identify the poisonous illiberalism of Critical Orthodoxy. Readers of these works will know where "wokeism" comes from and why Critical Thinkers interpret the world in the way they do.

The next critical battle is understanding the mechanisms Critical Thinkers use to assume power – radical claims, language, and bureaucracy. This book addressed some of the way in which Critical Thinkers use these mechanisms, but it does not fully account for their vocabulary or methods.

To further decipher the language of Critical Thinkers, consider visiting the Social Justice Encyclopedia at New Discourses (newdiscourses.com). There you will find over 100 encyclopedia entries for the most popular terms and concepts used by Critical Thinkers. You will also find podcasts, articles, woke literature, and videos that explain Critical Social Justice Theory in plain English.

Critical Thinkers obfuscate language to coerce everyone into signing up to the revolutionary struggle. You don't have to buy a bunch of books or spend hours reading through special encyclopedia entries to combat the Woke Warpath, but you must, at a minimum, understand their key terms and concepts. Once you speak their language, you can distinguish between what they say and what they mean; between what they tell you they want to do and what they will actually do; between their fantasy and reality.

The second critical battle is applying what you have learned in this book and others to call out the incursions of Critical Thinkers as they happen. Critical Thinkers poison institutions, weaken their immune systems and infect them with Critical Orthodoxy. To stop the Woke Warpath, we must mount an antibody response that suffocates the Critical Thinker's neo-racism and neo-sexism with free speech and the truth.

I believed education was all but lost when I started writing this book. I could not have been more wrong. In 2021, parents all over the U.S. stood up to reject the Critical Orthodoxy that had captured their children's schools. There is much to learn from the anti-woke parent's movement that we can apply to other institutions as an antidote to the poisonous ideology of postmodern neo-Marxism.

The First Major Anti-Woke Victory

With Christopher Rufo's investigative reporting in hand, parents around the nation identified the practice of Critical Race Theory and Critical Pedagogy in their children's schools in 2021. These parents attended school board meetings en masse to protest against the programming of their children and take educators to task for their actions. The initial backlash was spectacular, with political pundits and Critical Thinkers claiming that these parents were nothing but right-wing zealots trying to start a culture war to protect institutional racism. The establishment hated the fact that parents had correctly identified Critical Race Theory and made it a household name, shining a light on the grooming of children nationwide.

Critical Thinkers first claimed that Critical Race Theory was just an obscure legal theory taught in graduate law schools. With mountains of evidence in hand, parents forced educators to acknowledge this was a blatant lie, and that CRT was being practiced in schools with children as young as five. Critical Thinkers then claimed that children weren't being taught Critical Race Theory – they were being taught "real history." Again, parents provided overwhelming evidence contradicting these claims, citing egregious examples of educators practicing counter-storytelling to force a false history on children. Backed into a corner, Critical Thinkers attempted a complete narrative shift, extolling just how essential CRT practice in the classroom really was. Not only did CRT now exist, but Critical Thinkers also considered it a cornerstone of K-12 education nationwide.

With the truth and momentum on their side, parents across the country pressured educators, school boards, and legislators to ban the teaching of race essentialism, collective guilt, and compulsory ways for children to talk. Dozens of states have moved to ban the teaching of CRT's core tenets, some more successfully than others. Many bills introduced to State legislatures intentionally do not prohibit the teaching of Critical Race Theory for fears that such actions will stifle discourse and deflate the marketplace of ideas. Instead, the most successful bills ban the teaching and practice of CRT's cornerstone principles.

1. That the United States or the state is "fundamentally and irredeemably racist or sexist";

2. That individuals are "inherently racist, sexist, or oppressive" by virtue of "race" or other intrinsic characteristics;

3. That individuals are personally "responsible for actions committed in the past by other members of the same" race or other intrinsic characteristics; and

4. That individuals' "moral character is necessarily determined" by race or other intrinsic characteristics.[243]

In banning CRT in schools, parents across the country are scoring the first major victories against the Woke Warpath. There are several lessons to be learned from this movement. The first and most important lesson is that free thinkers can win. Critical Thinkers do not occupy the moral high ground, regardless of what conspiratorial claims they make. By equipping ourselves with the ability to discern their true beliefs, actions, intentions, and practice, free thinkers can call out all of the lies and absurdities when they see them. Critical Thinkers rely on silence and fear. Do not be silent and do not be fearful. The jig is up; if we speak truth into the world, we will find that others are just as tired of the insanity and are willing to pick up the sword in defense of liberalism.

The second lesson is that you don't have to be on the front line to make a difference. The parents' movement against CRT has been so successful because everyday people were willing to pitch in to fight the Woke Warpath in whatever capacity they could. Some parents spoke at school board meetings, while others called legislators. Some offered to do administrative work, while others handled networking and managed social media groups. Some parents facilitated community conversations, read the relevant literature, provided public critiques of school curriculum, and were elected to school boards. One doesn't need to be the face of the movement –

one only needs to do what one is comfortable doing, and to support those who, for various reasons, can take a more public and invested stand against the Woke Warpath.

A third lesson the anti-CRT movement has taught us is that Critical Thinkers are often incompetent, and their true character and intentions emerge when they are pressed to defend their worldview. On September 29th, 2021, the National School Boards Association (NSBA) delivered a letter to President Biden, asking him to bring down the full power of the federal government on parents protesting the practice of CRT in their children's classrooms. The letter likened the pressure mounted on school boards "to a form of domestic terrorism," arguing that "critical race theory is not taught in public schools and remains a complex law school and graduate school subject."[244] It was later revealed that the NSBA had collaborated with both the Justice Department and the White House when drafting their letter.

When pressured, Critical Thinkers will lie until they are blue in the face, all the while relying on their incredible institutional power to silence dissidents. The National Education Association (NEA) is the largest union in the country, representing millions of educators. The NEA has explicitly called for its members to practice CRT, promising to defend any teacher brought to task for programming children to view the world through a race communist prism. Perhaps the NEA and the NSBA should have collaborated to ensure they didn't lose grip on their narratives. Parents around the country did not tolerate such threats and corruption well. Dozens of states have recently voted to withdraw from the NSBA completely. Many are calling for defunding the teacher's unions for the moral corruption and child abuse they so fervently defend.

Evergreen or evergreen?

The Critical Thinker believes that they have a moral obligation to compare and critique America against the ideal communistic society inside their head. They have developed a critical consciousness and they practice Critical Social Justice Theory, making it their life's mission to spread the practicing of Critical Thinking to others. They are a radical activist marching on the Woke Warpath, disrupting and dismantling everything to catalyze the revolution their worldview demands.

The Critical Thinker believes individualism is subordinate to group membership. They categorize people based on sex and race, placing social significance into identity categories to poison the liberal system. Although they cloak their maneuvers in progressive language, their fight for social justice is nothing more than a battle to redistribute freedom and power until they have all of it. To achieve this end, they will introduce radical claims, suffocate free speech, discard objectivity and reason, and corrupt the minds of those unsuspecting pawns they so carelessly sacrifice on the altar of justice.

History may not repeat, but it does rhyme. In 2022, the poetry of tyranny is far too recognizable. Hitler, Stalin, Mao, and Pol Pot placed social significance into identity categories to secure power and spark revolution. Hitler stamped the Jewish people with collective guilt, condemning millions through the power of counter-storytelling, using racial permanence to convince good people to do wicked things. Stalin used a similar playbook to demonize the kulaks in Ukraine, leading to the Holomodor and the starvation of millions. Not to be outdone, Mao's Great Leap Forward led to the deaths by starvation of roughly 50 million people. Pol Pot was a bit more direct – his Khmer Rouge would bury over a million dissidents in their Killing Fields. We mustn't be so ignorant as to believe that the results of such social justice movements would have been drastically different had we been in charge, leading the way with diversity, equity, and inclusion.

We know what happens when tyrants use identity politics to usurp power and fundamentally restructure society in accordance with their moral imperatives. Those responsible for the most reprehensible acts of the last century all believed themselves to be acting in the best interests of others – in the interest of justice. The fascists and communists of both the East and West thought power to be the fundamental organizing principle of society. They believed that intergroup differences were larger than intragroup differences, that corruption and privilege drive disparate outcomes between groups, and that any sufficiently equitable society would require significant redistribution of freedom. Even a cursory reading of history is sufficient to understand that any society that embraces group identity over the sacred individual is marked by the kinds of horror we can only wish humans were incapable of.

If Critical Thinkers are allowed to continue on the Woke Warpath the America we know will cease to exist. The damage she has sustained from the onslaught of Critical Social Justice is already sufficient to leave permanent scar tissue; but make no mistake, Critical Thinkers will not stop until they have decimated liberalism entirely. That is their explicit goal. That is their only purpose. Accompanied by thunderous applause, the last pillars will fall as Critical Thinkers celebrate their short-lived emancipation. For all of their Critical Thought, they do not know that the roof is coming down on their heads. If you value freedom, truth, and the individual – now is the moment to familiarize yourself with Western architecture. We haven't much time and there is much to rebuild.

NOTES

1. Ibram X. Kendi, *How to Be an Antiracist* (New York: One World, 2019).
2. Christopher F. Rufo et al., "Identity Politics in Cupertino, California Elementary School," City Journal, June 21, 2021, https://www.city-journal.org/identity-politics-in-cupertino-california-elementary-school.
3. Selim Algar and Kate Sheehy, "NYC Public School Asks Parents to 'Reflect' on Their 'Whiteness'," New York Post (New York Post, February 17, 2021), https://nypost.com/2021/02/16/nyc-public-school-asks-parents-to-reflect-on-their-whiteness/.
4. Christopher F. Rufo, "The New Segregation," Christopher F. Rufo, January 15, 2021, https://christopherrufo.com/the-new-segregation/.
5. Roger Kiska, "Antonio Gramsci's Long March through History," Acton Institute, accessed November 16, 2021, https://www.acton.org/religion-liberty/volume-29-number-3/antonio-gramscis-long-march-through-history.
6. Richard W Pogge, "Real-World Relativity: The GPS Navigation System," GPS and Relativity, March 11, 2017, http://www.astronomy.ohio-state.edu/~pogge/Ast162/Unit5/gps.html.
7. James Lindsay, "Critical Theory," New Discourses, July 9, 2021, https://newdiscourses.com/tftw-critical-theory/.
8. Mark Murphy, "'The More Justice, the Less Freedom': Max Horkheimer on Critical Theory," Social Theory Applied, accessed November 16, 2021, https://socialtheoryapplied.com/2014/10/03/4204/.
9. Herbert Marcuse, *An Essay on Liberation* (Estados Unidos: Beacon, 1969).
10. ibid
11. ibid

12. ibid
13. ibid
14. ibid
15. Pluckrose, Helen and James A., Lindsay. 2020. *Cynical Theories: How Activist Scholarship Made Everything About Race, Gender, and Identity-and Why This Harms Everybody.* Durham, North Carolina: Pitchstone Publishing.
16. "The Evergreen State College Developmental Aspects Prior to Appointment of the President," Evergreen State College Archives, accessed November 18, 2021, https://archives.evergreen.edu/1971/1971-01/clabaugh_doc.pdf.
17. Dr. Garrett Heyns, "Statement by Dr. Garrett Heyns, Olympia," Evergreen State College Archives, accessed November 18, 2021, https://archives.evergreen.edu/1971/1971-01/heyns_legaddress1967.pdf.
18. ibid
19. "The Evergreen State College Developmental Aspects Prior to Appointment of the President," Evergreen State College Archives, accessed November 18, 2021, https://archives.evergreen.edu/1971/1971-01/clabaugh_doc.pdf.
20. "America in Translation: History, Culture, Theory (Foundations in CTLWS)," The Evergreen State College, accessed November 18, 2021, https://www.evergreen.edu/catalog/offering/america-translation-history-culture-theory-foundations-ctlws-28546.
21. Katherine Long, "The Evergreen State College Looking to Shed Its 'Hippie' Reputation," YakimaHerald, accessed November 18, 2021, https://www.yakimaherald.com/news/state_news/the-evergreen-state-college-looking-to-shed-its-hippie-reputation/article_fea43534-bae3-59b9-a9ed-ee0e46cb5e87.html.
22. Michael Rietmulder, "Macklemore Talks Sounders Deal, Dave Meinert and Seattle Hip-Hop," The Seattle Times (The Seattle Times Company, October 24, 2019), https://www.seattletimes.com/entertainment/music/macklemore-talks-sounders-deal-dave-meinert-and-seattle-hip-hop/.
23. "George Bridges: Evergreen's next President," The Evergreen State College, accessed November 18, 2021, https://www.evergreen.edu/magazine/george-bridges-evergreens-next-president.
24. "President George Bridges: Initial Observations," YouTube (The Evergreen State College), accessed November 18, 2021, https://www.youtube.com/watch?v=CkwSW1ZLszo.

25. "Black Lives Matter Protesters Disrupt Bernie Sanders Rally," YouTube (CBS News), accessed November 18, 2021, https://www.youtube.com/watch?v=p2iMM7m12zE.
26. ibid
27. Dan Merica, "Black Lives Matter Protesters Shut down Sanders Event in Seattle | CNN Politics," CNN (Cable News Network, August 10, 2015), https://www.cnn.com/2015/08/08/politics/bernie-sanders-black-lives-matter-protesters/.
28. Michael Martinez, "Who Is Kim Davis, Kentucky Clerk Jailed over Same-Sex Marriage Licenses?" CNN (Cable News Network, September 8, 2015), https://www.cnn.com/2015/09/04/us/kim-davis-things-to-know/index.html.
29. Revolt Revolt, "Baltimore to Pay Freddie Gray Family $6.4 Million in Settlement," REVOLT (REVOLT, September 14, 2015), https://www.revolt.tv/2015/9/14/20814356/baltimore-to-pay-freddie-gray-family-6-4-million-in-settlement.
30. "Launching Evergreen's Equity Canoe," YouTube (Benjamin A. Boyce), accessed November 18, 2021, https://www.youtube.com/watch?v=E7jttvGNJlg.
31. ibid
32. "Dumbing Data down at Evergreen," YouTube (Benjamin A. Boyce), accessed November 18, 2021, https://www.youtube.com/watch?v=qTVl5OwnvU4.
33. ibid
34. "Race and Pedagogy National Conference 2014 Program," University of Puget Sound (University of Puget Sound), accessed November 18, 2021, https://soundideas.pugetsound.edu/cgi/viewcontent.cgi?article=1021&context=race_pedagogy.
35. "Coming Together Speaker Series: Dr. Robin DiAngelo," YouTube (The Evergreen State College Productions), accessed November 18, 2021, https://www.youtube.com/watch?v=wVddM1hzmvI.
36. The Council, "The Council: Initial Meeting," Evergreen State College, accessed November 18, 2021, https://www.evergreen.edu/sites/default/files/equity/documents/16.04.27%20Equity%20Council%20Meeting%20Agenda.pdf.
37. ibid
38. "Strategic Equity Plan," YouTube, accessed April 18, 2021, https://www.youtube.com/?gl=DE.

39. ibid
40. ibid
41. ibid
42. ibid
43. ibid
44. ibid
45. ibid
46. "Correspondence between Bret Weinstein and Rashida Love," Committee Schedules, Agendas, and Documents, accessed November 18, 2021, https://app.leg.wa.gov/committeeschedules.
47. Cooper Point Journal, "Day of Absence Changes Form," The Cooper Point Journal, April 11, 2017, http://www.cooperpointjournal.com/2017/04/10/day-of-absence-changes-form/.
48. "Correspondence between Bret Weinstein and Rashida Love," Committee Schedules, Agendas, and Documents, accessed November 18, 2021, https://app.leg.wa.gov/committeeschedules.
49. Elliot Kaufman, "Another Professor, Another Mob," National Review (National Review, May 26, 2017), https://www.nationalreview.com/2017/05/evergreen-state-pc-mob-accosts-liberal-professor/.
50. "2017 Day of Absence On-Campus Schedule," Committee Schedules, Agendas, and Documents, accessed November 18, 2021, https://www.evergreen.edu/sites/default/files/2017DoA_OnCampus_Schedule.pdf.
51. "Part Two: Teaching to Transgress," YouTube (Mike Nayna, March 6, 2019), https://www.youtube.com/watch?v=A0W9QbkX8Cs.
52. ibid
53. ibid
54. ibid
55. ibid
56. ibid
57. ibid
58. Cooper Point Journal, "Students Demand Change," The Cooper Point Journal, accessed November 19, 2021, https://www.cooperpointjournal.com/2017/05/27/complete-list-of-student-demands/.
59. "Part Three: The Hunted Individual," YouTube (Mike Nayna), accessed November 19, 2021, https://www.youtube.com/watch?v=2vyBLCqyUes.
60. ibid

61. "Part Three: The Hunted Individual," YouTube (Mike Nayna), accessed November 19, 2021, https://www.youtube.com/watch?v=2vyBLCqyUes.
62. Joe Sterling, "Classes at Washington College Canceled Again amid threats - CNN," June 5, 2017, https://www.cnn.com/2017/06/05/us/washington-evergreen-classes-canceled/index.html.
63. Marla Milling, "Johnson & Johnson Announces New Band-AIDS, but That Can't Fix Racial Inequality," Forbes (Forbes Magazine, June 16, 2020), https://www.forbes.com/sites/marlamilling/2020/06/15/johnson--johnson-announces-new-band-aids-but-that-cant-fix-racial-inequality/?sh=432c71016e7d.
64. Johnson & Johnson, "Johnson & Johnson," Content Lab U.S., November 17, 2020, https://www.jnj.com/johnson-johnson-to-address-racial-and-social-injustice-through-platform-that-aims-to-eliminate-health-inequities-for-people-of-color.
65. "Racism," Merriam-Webster (Merriam-Webster), accessed November 15, 2021, https://www.merriam-webster.com/dictionary/racism.
66. Robin DiAngelo, "Anti-Racism Handout - Robin DiAngelo," RobinDiAngelo.com, accessed December 3, 2021, https://robindiangelo.com/wp-content/uploads/2016/06/Anti-racism-handout-1-page-2016.pdf.
67. Ibram X. Kendi, "Ibram X. Kendi Defines What It Means to Be an Antiracist," Penguin Books UK, June 10, 2020, https://www.penguin.co.uk/articles/2020/june/ibram-x-kendi-definition-of-antiracist.html.
68. James Lindsay, "Diversity," New Discourses, August 31, 2021, https://newdiscourses.com/tftw-diversity/.
69. "Queensborough Community College," Website for Queensborough Community College, accessed November 15, 2021, https://www.qcc.cuny.edu/diversity/definition.html.
70. James Lindsay, "Ways of Knowing," New Discourses, April 5, 2021, https://newdiscourses.com/tftw-ways-of-knowing/.
71. Erika D Smith, "Column: Larry Elder Is the Black Face of White Supremacy. You've Been Warned," Los Angeles Times (Los Angeles Times, August 20, 2021), https://www.latimes.com/california/story/2021-08-20/recall-candidate-larry-elder-is-a-threat-to-black-californians.
72. Holly Martinez, "Equity vs. Equality: What's The Difference - Examples & Definitions," United Way NCA, September 21, 2021, https://unitedwaynca.org/stories/equity-vs-equality/.
73. Conor Friedersdorf, "Witnesses Saw Michael Brown Attacking–and Others Saw Him Giving Up," The Atlantic (Atlantic Media Company, November

25, 2014), https://www.theatlantic.com/national/archive/2014/11/major-contradictions-in-eyewitness-accounts-of-michael-Browns-death/383157/.

74. ibid

75. "President Obama on Ferguson Shooting & Protests (C-Span) - YouTube" (C-Span, August 14, 2014), https://www.youtube.com/watch?v=ZKd7tx78fvY.

76. Scott Neuman, "Ferguson Timeline: Grief, Anger and Tension," NPR (NPR, November 24, 2014), https://www.npr.org/sections/thetwo-way/2014/11/24/364103735/ferguson-timeline-grief-anger-and-tension.

77. Ray Sanchez, "Michael Brown's Stepfather: 'Burn This Bitch down!' | CNN," CNN (CNN, December 8, 2014), https://www.cnn.com/2014/11/25/us/michael-brown-stepfather-video/index.html.

78. Eyder Peralta and Bill Chappell, "Ferguson Jury: No Charges for Officer in Michael Brown's Death," NPR (NPR, November 24, 2014), https://www.npr.org/sections/thetwo-way/2014/11/24/366370100/grand-jury-reaches-decision-in-michael-brown-case?refresh=true%3Frefresh.

79. Heather Smith, "Meet the Bart-Stopping Woman behind 'Black Lives Matter,'" Grist, December 4, 2014, https://grist.org/politics/stopping-a-bart-train-in-michael-browns-name/.

80. "Fatal Force: Police Shootings Database," The Washington Post (WP Company), accessed November 15, 2021, https://www.washingtonpost.com/graphics/investigations/police-shootings-database/.

81. Associated Press, "Florida Deputies Shoot, Kill Man Who 'Motioned for a Gun,' Sheriff Says," WKMG (WKMG News 6 & ClickOrlando, December 9, 2020), https://www.clickorlando.com/news/florida/2020/12/09/florida-deputies-shoot-kill-man-who-motioned-for-a-gun-sheriff-says/.

82. Kellie Cowan, "Attempted Arrest Leads to Crash, Deadly Deputy-Involved Shooting at Busy Riverview Intersection, Sheriff Says," FOX 13 Tampa Bay (FOX 13 Tampa Bay, December 9, 2020), https://www.fox13news.com/news/attempted-arrest-leads-to-crash-deadly-deputy-involved-shooting-at-busy-riverview-intersection-sheriff-says.

83. Eric Levenson, "Former Officer Knelt on George Floyd for 9 Minutes and 29 Seconds -- Not the Infamous 8:46," CNN (Cable News Network, March 30, 2021), https://www.cnn.com/2021/03/29/us/george-floyd-timing-929-846/index.html.

84. "Raw Video: Officer Dustin Dillard's Bodycam Shows In-Custody Death of Tony Timpa - YouTube," YouTube (WFAA, August 2, 2019), https://www.youtube.com/watch?v=6X4PUwrq8tA.

85. Cary Aspinwall and Dave Boucher, "'You're Gonna Kill Me!': Dallas Police Body Cam Footage Reveals the Final Minutes of Tony Timpa's Life," The Dallas Morning News (The Dallas Morning News, August 20, 2019), https://www.dallasnews.com/news/investigations/2019/07/31/you-re-gonna-kill-me-dallas-police-body-cam-footage-reveals-the-final-minutes-of-tony-timpa-s-life/.
86. Rachel Treisman, "13-Year-Old Boy with Autism Disorder Shot by Salt Lake City Police," NPR (NPR, September 9, 2020), https://www.npr.org/2020/09/09/910975499/autistic-13-year-old-boy-shot-by-salt-lake-city-police.
87. Skylar Baker-Jordan, "A White Teen Was Killed by Cops. Working Class Lives Need to Matter, Too: Opinion," Newsweek (Newsweek, July 6, 2021), https://www.newsweek.com/white-teen-was-killed-cops-working-class-lives-need-matter-too-opinion-1607137.
88. Kellie Cowan, "Attempted Arrest Leads to Crash, Deadly Deputy-Involved Shooting at Busy Riverview Intersection, Sheriff Says," FOX 13 Tampa Bay (FOX 13 Tampa Bay, December 9, 2020), https://www.fox13news.com/news/attempted-arrest-leads-to-crash-deadly-deputy-involved-shooting-at-busy-riverview-intersection-sheriff-says.
89. "Fatal Force: Police Shootings Database," The Washington Post (WP Company), accessed November 15, 2021, https://www.washingtonpost.com/graphics/investigations/police-shootings-database/.
90. Julie Moreno, "Father of Kameron Prescott Shares Heartbreaking Details of 6-Year-Old's Shooting Death by Deputies," KSAT (KSAT San Antonio, December 3, 2019), https://www.ksat.com/news/local/2019/12/02/i-want-to-know-why-kameron-prescotts-father-shares-heartbreaking-details-of-6-year-olds-shooting-death-by-deputies/.
91. "Fatal Force: Police Shootings Database," The Washington Post (WP Company), accessed November 15, 2021, https://www.washingtonpost.com/graphics/investigations/police-shootings-database/.
92. "Crime in Arizona 2017 - Arizona Department of Public Safety," Arizona Department of Public Safety (Arizona Department of Public Safety), accessed November 15, 2021, https://www.azdps.gov/sites/default/files/media/FINAL_Crime_in_Arizona_2017_0.pdf.
93. "Wisconsin Department of Justice," UCR Arrest Demographics | Wisconsin Department of Justice (Wisconsin Department of Justice), accessed November 15, 2021, https://www.doj.state.wi.us/dles/bjia/ucr-arrest-demographics.

94. "State-by-State Data," The Sentencing Project (The Sentencing Project, July 28, 2020), https://www.sentencingproject.org/the-facts/#detail?state1Option=Alabama&state2Option=Iowa.

95. Christine Hauser, "Chicago Reels as 3 Children Are Gunned down in 4 Days," The New York Times (The New York Times, February 15, 2017), https://www.nytimes.com/2017/02/15/us/toddler-killed-chicago-murder.html.

96. Evelyn Holmes, "Chicago Shooting: 1-Month-Old Shot in Head among 7 Wounded in Englewood," ABC7 Chicago (WLS-TV, July 2, 2021), https://abc7chicago.com/chicago-shooting-englewood-baby-shot-mass/10852857/.

97. "Chicago Police Department," Chicago Police Department, accessed November 15, 2021, https://home.chicagopolice.org/wp-content/uploads/2019/03/Chicago-Police-Department-Annual-Report-2017.pdf.

98. "Table 43," FBI (FBI, September 17, 2018), https://ucr.fbi.gov/crime-in-the-u.s/2017/crime-in-the-u.s.-2017/tables/table-43.

99. "Crime in the U.S. - Expanded Homicide Data Table 3," FBI (FBI), accessed November 15, 2021, https://ucr.fbi.gov/crime-in-the-u.s/.

100. Osagie K. Obasogie, "Perspective | Police Killing Black People Is a Pandemic, Too," The Washington Post (WP Company, June 5, 2020), https://www.washingtonpost.com/outlook/police-violence-pandemic/2020/06/05/e1a2a1b0-a669-11ea-b619-3f9133bbb482_story.html.

101. Alana Semuels, "No, Most Black People Don't Live in Poverty-or Inner Cities," The Atlantic (Atlantic Media Company, October 14, 2016), https://www.theatlantic.com/business/archive/2016/10/trump-african-american-inner-city/503744/.

102. "Crime in the U.S. - Table 55," FBI (FBI), accessed November 15, 2021, https://ucr.fbi.gov/crime-in-the-u.s/2017/crime-in-the-u.s.-2017/tables/table-55.

103. "Crime in the U.S. - Table 29," FBI (FBI), accessed November 15, 2021, https://ucr.fbi.gov/crime-in-the-u.s/2017/crime-in-the-u.s.-2017/topic-pages/tables/table-29.

104. ibid

105. Jennifer A. Richeson, "Americans Are Determined to Believe in Black Progress," The Atlantic (Atlantic Media Company, July 27, 2020), https://www.theatlantic.com/magazine/archive/2020/09/the-mythology-of-racial-progress/614173/.

106. Myron Medcalf, "Duke's Mike Krzyzewski: 'Black Lives Matter' a Human Rights Statement, Not a Political One,"

ESPN (ESPN Internet Ventures, June 26, 2020), https://www.espn.com/mens-college-basketball/story/_/id/29371614/black-lives-matter-human-rights-statement-not-political-one.

107. Sam Levin, "Minneapolis Lawmakers Vow to Disband Police Department in Historic Move," The Guardian (Guardian News and Media, June 8, 2020), https://www.theguardian.com/us-news/2020/jun/07/minneapolis-city-council-defund-police-george-floyd.
108. "Community Safety and Violence Prevention Charter ... - Lims," Minneapolis MN (Minneapolis City Council), accessed November 16, 2021, https://lims.minneapolismn.gov/Download/File/3866/MPD%20Charter%20Amendment_VII%20062420%20Final.pdf.
109. "Board Index," Immediate Reinvestment & Long Term Change plan [budget] (Austin City Council), accessed November 16, 2021, https://austincouncilforum.org/viewtopic.php?t=1327.
110. "Resolution No. 20200611-050," The City of Austin (austintexas.gov), accessed November 16, 2021, https://www.austintexas.gov/edims/document.cfm?id=342178.
111. SFGTV, "Mayor London Breed City Budget Announcement July 31, 2020," YouTube (SFGovTv, July 31, 2020), https://www.youtube.com/watch?v=IrH9yUw8Res.
112. Sam Levin, "These US Cities Defunded Police: 'We're Transferring Money to the Community'," The Guardian (Guardian News and Media, March 11, 2021), https://www.theguardian.com/us-news/2021/mar/07/us-cities-defund-police-transferring-money-community.
113. Pamela Ugwudike, *An Introduction to Critical Criminology*, pg. 81 (Bristol, UK: Policy Press, 2015).
114. David O Brown, "For Immediate Release," News Release (Chicago Police Department), accessed November 16, 2021, https://home.chicagopolice.org/wp-content/uploads/26-May-21-Foot-Pursuit-Policy-1.pdf.
115. "State's Attorney, Mayor's Office, and Community Partners Announce Success of Covid Criminal Justice Policies," The Baltimore City State's Attorney's Office, accessed November 16, 2021, https://www.stattorney.org/media-center/press-releases/2243-state-s-attorney-mayor-s-office-and-community-partners-announce-success-of-covid-criminal-justice-policies.
116. Ray Sanchez et al., "US Police 'Very Nervous' about Officer-Initiated Enforcement as Gun Violence Soars," CNN (Cable News Network, June 23, 2021), https://www.cnn.com/2021/06/19/us/proactive-policing-stepping-back/index.html.

117. SkyNewsAustralia, "Guy 'Munching on Noodles' Rebuts CNN's Chris Cuomo's 'Polite Protest' Conundrum," YouTube (YouTube, June 18, 2020), https://www.youtube.com/watch?v=R0T3tajeWzk.

118. Stacey Vanek Smith, "Riots That Followed Anti-Racism Protests Come at Great Cost to Black-Owned Businesses," NPR (NPR, August 12, 2020), https://www.npr.org/2020/08/12/901859883/riots-that-followed-anti-racism-protests-come-at-great-cost-to-black-owned-busin.

119. Zachary Crockett, "3 Stories of Black-Owned Businesses Damaged in the Riots," The Hustle, June 6, 2020, https://thehustle.co/black-owned-businesses-riots-george-floyd/.

120. Susannah Cullinane, "Retired St. Louis Police Captain Killed after Responding to a Pawnshop Alarm during Looting," CNN (Cable News Network, August 27, 2020), https://www.cnn.com/2020/06/03/us/david-dorn-st-louis-police-shot-trnd/index.html.

121. Justin L. Mack and Elizabeth DePompei, "Chris Beaty Homicide: Suspect Charged with May Murder of 'Mr. Indianapolis'," The Indianapolis Star (Indianapolis Star, December 3, 2020), https://www.indystar.com/story/news/crime/2020/12/03/chris-beaty-homicide-suspect-charged-murder-may-shooting/3808044001/.

122. Special Reports, "Hands-off Patrol," Reuters (Thomson Reuters, September 13, 2021), https://www.reuters.com/investigates/special-report/usa-policing-minneapolis/.

123. ibid

124. Marielle Mohs, "With 5 Kids Shot in North Minneapolis in 2 Months, Community Begs for Halt to Gun Violence," WCCO | CBS Minnesota (WCCO | CBS Minnesota, July 11, 2021), https://minnesota.cbslocal.com/2021/07/11/lawlessness-has-taken-over-north-minneapolis-leaders-neighbors-beg-for-gun-violence-to-end/.

125. Jeff Asher, "Murder Rose by Almost 30% in 2020. It's Rising at a Slower Rate in 2021," The New York Times (The New York Times, September 22, 2021), https://www.nytimes.com/2021/09/22/upshot/murder-rise-2020.html.

126. David Pyrooz, Scott Wolfe, and Justin Nix, "Opinion: Understanding Denver's Devastating Rise in Homicides in 2020, the Largest in at Least 5 Years," NewsBreak (NewsBreak, February 24, 2021), https://www.newsbreak.com/news/2169865530390/opinion-understanding-denver-s-devastating-rise-in-homicides-in-2020-the-largest-in-at-least-5-years.

127. ibid

128. Jenny Gross and John Eligon, "Minneapolis City Council Votes to Remove $8 Million from Police Budget," The New York Times (The New York Times, December 10, 2020), https://www.nytimes.com/2020/12/10/us/minneapolis-police-funding.html.

129. Admin, "How Much Did the 2021 Adopted Budget Reduce Spending For the New York City Police Department?" New York City by the numbers (New York City Independent Budget Office, August 18, 2020), https://ibo.nyc.ny.us/cgi-park2/2020/08/how-much-did-the-2021-adopted-budget-reduce-spending-for-the-new-york-city-police-department/.

130. CBSLA Staff, "'We Can't Guarantee Your Safety': Head of LAPD's Police Officers' Union Warns Tourists Away," CBS Los Angeles (CBS Los Angeles, December 7, 2021), https://losangeles.cbslocal.com/2021/12/07/we-cant-guarantee-your-safety-head-of-lapds-police-officers-union-warns-tourists-away/.

131. Logan Wroge, "West High School to Test 'Grading Floor' as Part of District Examination of Freshman Grading," madison.com (madison.com, November 19, 2019), https://madison.com/wsj/news/local/education/local_schools/west-high-school-to-test-grading-floor-as-part-of-district-examination-of-freshman-grading/article_d9a941e6-f7e8-54f2-86b9-92083c1c5c35.html.

132. Hillary Borrud, "Gov. Kate Brown Signed a Law to Allow Oregon Students to Graduate without Proving They Can Write or Do Math. She Doesn't Want to Talk about It.," oregonlive, accessed November 16, 2021, https://www.oregonlive.com/politics/2021/08/gov-kate-brown-signed-a-law-to-allow-oregon-students-to-graduate-without-proving-they-can-write-or-do-math-she-doesnt-want-to-talk-about-it.html.

133. Coleen McMurray, "Achievement Gap: Public Doesn't Blame Schools," Gallup.com (Gallup, September 2, 2021), https://news.gallup.com/poll/9625/achievement-gap-public-doesnt-blame-schools.aspx.

134. Ibram X. Kendi, "Why the Academic Achievement Gap Is a Racist Idea," AAIHS (AAIHS, October 20, 2016), https://www.aaihs.org/why-the-academic-achievement-gap-is-a-racist-idea/.

135. Sean F Reardon, "The Widening Academic Achievement Gap Between the Rich and the Poor: New Evidence and Possible Explanations," Stanford University (Stanford University), accessed November 16, 2021, https://archive.org/details/perma_cc_KAD5-PBEY.

136. Timothy Smeeding et al., "Chapter 6," in *Persistence, Privilege, and Parenting: The Comparative Study of Intergenerational Mobility* (New York: Russell Sage Foundation, 2011).

137. Ron Haskins, "Three Simple Rules Poor Teens Should Follow to Join the Middle Class," Brookings (Brookings, July 28, 2016), https://www.brookings.edu/opinions/three-simple-rules-poor-teens-should-follow-to-join-the-middle-class/.

138. Elizabeth Wildsmith, Jennifer Manlove, and Elizabeth Cook, "Dramatic Increase in the Proportion of Births Outside of Marriage in the United States from 1990 to 2016," Child Trends, accessed November 16, 2021, https://www.childtrends.org/publications/dramatic-increase-in-percentage-of-births-outside-marriage-among-whites-Browns-and-women-with-higher-education-levels.

139. DOUGLAS B. DOWNEY, "The School Performance of Children from Single-Mother and Single-Father Families:" *Journal of Family Issues* 15, no. 1 (1994): pp. 129-147, https://doi.org/10.1177/019251394015001006.

140. Annette Lareau, *Unequal Childhoods: Class, Race, and Family Life* (Berkeley, Calif: University of California Press, 2014).

141. Jill Gilkerson et al., "Mapping the Early Language Environment Using All-Day Recordings and Automated Analysis," ASHA Wire (American Journal of Speech Language Pathology), accessed November 16, 2021, https://pubs.asha.org/doi/10.1044/2016_AJSLP-15-0169.

142. Norbert Schady, "Parents' Education, Mothers' Vocabulary, and Cognitive Development in Early Childhood: Longitudinal Evidence from Ecuador," American journal of public health (American Public Health Association, December 2011), https://www.ncbi.nlm.nih.gov/pmc/articles/PMC3222428/.

143. Paul DiPerna and Michael Shaw, "2018 Schooling in America," EdChoice (EdChoice), accessed November 16, 2021, https://www.edchoice.org/wp-content/uploads/2018/12/2018-12-Schooling-In-America-by-Paul-DiPerna-and-Michael-Shaw.pdf.

144. Sheila Murray and Kim S Rueben, "Racial Disparities in Education Finance: Going beyond Equal Revenues," Tax Policy Center (Tax Policy Center, November 3, 2008), https://www.taxpolicycenter.org/publications/racial-disparities-education-finance-going-beyond-equal-revenues/full.

145. "Per Pupil Expenditures: Georgia," Office of Elementary & Secondary Education (Department of Education), accessed November 16, 2021, https://oese.ed.gov/ppe/georgia/.

146. ibid

147. "The Educational Opportunity Project at Stanford: Home," The Educational Opportunity Project at Stanford University, accessed November 16, 2021, https://edopportunity.org/.

148. ibid

149. "Discipline Reform through the Eyes of Teachers: Statistics, Charts, Tables & Quotes: Thomas B. Fordham Institute Advancing Educational Excellence," Discipline Reform Through the Eyes of Teachers: 2019 Statistics, Charts, Tables & Quotes (Thomas B. Fordham Institute Advancing Educational Excellence), accessed November 16, 2021, http://teachersondiscipline.com/#student-behavior-problems.

150. ibid

151. Paul DiPerna and Michael Shaw, "2018 Schooling in America," EdChoice (EdChoice), accessed November 16, 2021, https://www.edchoice.org/wp-content/uploads/2018/12/2018-12-Schooling-In-America-by-Paul-DiPerna-and-Michael-Shaw.pdf.

152. Eric Kaufmann et al., "Safe and Orderly Schools: Updated Guidance on School Discipline," Manhattan Institute, March 14, 2019, https://www.manhattan-institute.org/dear-colleague-letter-school-discipline.

153. "Disruptive Behavior Results," Buffalo Teachers Federation, accessed November 16, 2021, http://www.btfny.org/press/disruptive_behavior_results_2018.pdf.

154. ibid

155. "The Educational Opportunity Project at Stanford," Opportunity Explorer | The Educational Opportunity Project at Stanford University, accessed November 16, 2021, https://edopportunity.org/explorer/#/map/none/counties/avg/ses/wb/5.87/28.39/-84.91/12033,30.865,-87.446.

156. "Escambia County FL School District Superintendent Tim Smith- White People Bad?" YouTube (Larry ForReal, August 9, 2021), https://www.youtube.com/watch?v=3ubRqR90V2w.

157. "The Condition of Education 2021," National Center for Education Statistics, accessed November 16, 2021, https://nces.ed.gov/pubs2020/2020144.pdf.

158. ibid

159. ibid

160. ibid

161. DoDEA Communications, "Dodea Schools Best in the U.S. On Nation's Report Card," DoDEA, accessed November 16, 2021, https://www.dodea.edu/newsroom/pressreleases/naep-2019.cfm.

162. Paul Rossi, "I Refuse to Stand by While My Students Are Indoctrinated," Common Sense with Bari Weiss (Common Sense

with Bari Weiss, April 13, 2021), https://bariweiss.substack.com/p/i-refuse-to-stand-by-while-my-students.

163. "Dignity & Belonging," GCS Dignity & Belonging, accessed November 16, 2021, https://www.gcschool.org/programs/dignity-and-belonging.

164. Paul Rossi, "I Refuse to Stand by While My Students Are Indoctrinated," Common Sense with Bari Weiss (Common Sense with Bari Weiss, April 13, 2021), https://bariweiss.substack.com/p/i-refuse-to-stand-by-while-my-students.

165. "Culturally Responsive & Sustaining Pedagogy Westerly High School August 31, 2021," Judicial Watch, accessed November 16, 2021, https://www.judicialwatch.org/wp-content/uploads/2021/10/Rhode-Island-CRT-Teacher-training-September-2021-1.pdf.

166. Christopher Rufo, "Radicals in the Classroom," Christopher F. Rufo, January 14, 2021, https://christopherrufo.com/radicals-in-the-classroom/.

167. ibid

168. Douglass Kellner, "Marxian Perspectives on Educational Philosophy: From Classical Marxism to Critical Pedagogy," UCLA School of Education & Informational Studies, accessed November 16, 2021, https://pages.gseis.ucla.edu/faculty/kellner/papers/marxed.htm.

169. Paulo Freire, *Pedagogy of the Oppressed* (New York, NY: The Continuum International Publishing Group Ltd., 1993).

170. McKenzie KB, Christman DE, Hernandez F, et al. From the Field: A Proposal for Educating Leaders for Social Justice. *Educational Administration Quarterly.* 2008;44(1):111-138.

171. Gloria Ladson-Billings, "Just What Is Critical Race Theory and What's It Doing in a Nice Field like Education?" The University of Arizona, accessed November 16, 2021, https://www.best-schools.info/just-what-is-critical-race-theory/.

172. ibid

173. Richard Delgado and Jean Stefancic, *Critical Race Theory: An Introduction* (New York: New York University Press, 2001), 2.

174. Richard Delgado and Jean Stefancic, *Critical Race Theory: An Introduction* (New York: New York University Press, 2001), 3.

175. Richard Delgado and Jean Stefancic, *Critical Race Theory: An Introduction* (New York: New York University Press, 2001), 3.

176. Richard Delgado and Jean Stefancic, *Critical Race Theory: An Introduction* (New York: New York University Press, 2001), 3.

177. Richard Delgado and Jean Stefancic, *Critical Race Theory: An Introduction* (New York: New York University Press, 2001), 3.

178. Richard Delgado and Jean Stefancic, *Critical Race Theory: An Introduction* (New York: New York University Press, 2001), 3.

179. Gloria Ladson-Billings, "Critical Race Theory-What It Is Not!," Routledge Handbooks Online (Routledge Handbooks Online, September 2, 2013), https://www.routledgehandbooks.com/doi/10.4324/9780203155721.ch3.

180. Gloria Ladson-Billings, "Just What Is Critical Race Theory and What's It Doing in a Nice Field like Education?" The University of Arizona, accessed November 16, 2021, https://www.best-schools.info/just-what-is-critical-race-theory/.

181. Gloria Ladson-Billings, "Just What Is Critical Race Theory and What's It Doing in a Nice Field like Education?" The University of Arizona, accessed November 16, 2021, https://www.best-schools.info/just-what-is-critical-race-theory/.

182. Gloria Ladson-Billings, "Just What Is Critical Race Theory and What's It Doing in a Nice Field like Education?" The University of Arizona, accessed November 16, 2021, https://www.best-schools.info/just-what-is-critical-race-theory/.

183. Sonia M Cintron, Dani Wadlington, and Andre ChenFang, "A Pathway to Equitable Math Instruction Dismantling Racism in Mathematics Instruction," equitablemath.org, accessed November 16, 2021, https://equitablemath.org/wp-content/uploads/sites/2/2020/11/1_STRIDE1.pdf.

184. ibid

185. ibid

186. ibid

187. ibid

188. ibid

189. "Trans-Atlantic Slave Trade - Database," Slave Voyages, accessed November 16, 2021, https://www.slavevoyages.org/voyage/database.

190. William E Simon and Kay S Hymowitz, "Uniquely Bad-but Not Uniquely American," City Journal, October 16, 2020, https://www.city-journal.org/slavery-failure-of-1619-project.

191. Christopher F. Rufo et al., "Identity Politics in Cupertino, California Elementary School," City Journal, June 21, 2021, https://www.city-journal.org/identity-politics-in-cupertino-california-elementary-school.

192. Christopher F Rufo, "Buffalo Public Schools' Critical Race Theory Curriculum," City Journal, June 21, 2021, https://www.city-journal.org/buffalo-public-schools-critical-race-theory-curriculum.
193. Christopher F Rufo, "Critical Race Theory in Wake County, NC Schools," City Journal, March 17, 2021, https://www.city-journal.org/critical-race-theory-in-wake-county-nc-schools.
194. "California School Dashboard," California School Dashboard (CA dept of education), accessed November 16, 2021, https://www.caschooldashboard.org/reports/38684783833407/2020.
195. CACAGNY, "CACAGNY's Statement Denouncing Mayor Bill De Blasio's Decision to Eliminate NYC's Gifted and Talented Program to Dumb down Children for 'Equity.'," Twitter (Twitter), accessed November 16, 2021, https://twitter.com/cacagny.
196. https://blog.google/outreach-initiatives/diversity/getting-to-work-on-diversity-at-google/
197. https://about.fb.com/news/2014/06/building-a-more-diverse-facebook/
198. https://web.archive.org/web/20140812164241/https://www.apple.com/diversity/
199. Frame Shift Consulting, "Welcome to the Online Ally Skills Workshop!" Frame Shift Consulting, accessed January 7, 2022, https://files.frameshiftconsulting.com/Ally%20Skills%20Workshop%20slides.pdf.
200. James Damore, "Google's Ideological Echo Chamber," DocumentCloud, accessed January 7, 2022, https://www.documentcloud.org/documents/3914586-Googles-Ideological-Echo-Chamber.
201. Sundar Pichai, "Note to Employees from CEO Sundar Pichai," Google (Google, August 8, 2017), https://blog.google/outreach-initiatives/diversity/note-employees-ceo-sundar-pichai/.
202. Brenda K. Todd et al., "Sex Differences in Children's Toy Preferences: A Systematic Review, Meta-Regression, and Meta-Analysis," Wiley Online Library (John Wiley & Sons, Ltd, November 22, 2017), https://onlinelibrary.wiley.com/doi/abs/10.1002/icd.2064.
203. ibid
204. Janice M Hassett, Erin R Siebert, and Kim Wallen, "Sex Differences in Rhesus Monkey Toy Preferences Parallel Those of Children," Hormones and behavior (U.S. National Library of Medicine, August 2008), https://www.ncbi.nlm.nih.gov/pmc/articles/PMC2583786/.
205. Rong Su, James Rounds, and Patrick Ian Armstrong, "Men and Things, Women and People: A Meta-Analysis of Sex Differences in Interests,"

PubMed.gov (U.S. National Library of Medicine), accessed January 7, 2022, https://pubmed.ncbi.nlm.nih.gov/19883140/.

206. ibid

207. R Lynn and T Martin, "Gender Differences in Extraversion, Neuroticism, and Psychoticism in 37 Nations," PubMed.gov (U.S. National Library of Medicine), accessed January 7, 2022, https://pubmed.ncbi.nlm.nih.gov/9200973/.

208. Johnny Wood, "These 4 Nordic Countries Hold the Secret to Gender Equality," World Economic Forum, accessed January 7, 2022, https://www.weforum.org/agenda/2018/12/nordic-countries-women-equality-gender-pay-gap-2018/.

209. Hayley Halpin, "'A Gender Equality Paradox': Countries with More Gender Equality Have Fewer Female Stem Grads," TheJournal.ie, accessed January 7, 2022, https://www.thejournal.ie/gender-equality-countries-stem-girls-3848156-Feb2018/.

210. NBC News, "Read: Democratic Debate Transcript, November 20, 2019," NBCNews.com (NBCUniversal News Group, November 21, 2019), https://www.nbcnews.com/politics/2020-election/read-democratic-debate-transcript-november-20-2019-n1088186.

211. Valentin Bolotnyy and Natalia Emanuel, "Why Do Women Earn Less than Men ... - Scholars at Harvard," Harvard Scholar, accessed January 7, 2022, https://scholar.harvard.edu/files/bolotnyy/files/be_gendergap.pdf.

212. ibid

213. "About Us," Project Implicit, accessed November 17, 2021, https://implicit.harvard.edu/implicit/aboutus.html.

214. "About the IAT," Project Implicit, accessed November 17, 2021, https://www.projectimplicit.net/resources/about-the-iat/.

215. Simone de Beauvoir, *The Second Sex* (New York: Vintage, 2011).

216. Judith Butler, *Gender Trouble: Feminism and the Subversion of Identity* (New York; London: Routledge, 2006).

217. ibid

218. OpIndia Staff, "Canadian Man Jailed for Calling His Biologically Female Child as 'Daughter'," OpIndia, March 18, 2021, https://www.opindia.com/2021/03/canadian-man-jailed-for-calling-his-biologically-female-child-as-daughter/.

219. "2017 Plastic Surgery Statistics Report," American Society of Plastic Surgeons (American Society of Plastic Surgeons), accessed November 17,

2021, https://www.plasticsurgery.org/documents/News/Statistics/2017/body-contouring-gender-confirmation-2017.pdf.

220. Abigail Shrier, "Gender Activists Are Trying to Cancel My Book. Why Is Silicon Valley Helping Them?" Quillette (Quillette, November 19, 2020), https://quillette.com/2020/11/07/gender-activists-are-trying-to-cancel-my-book-why-is-silicon-valley-helping-them/.

221. ibid

222. Hillel Italie, "Booksellers Association Apologizes for Anti-Trans Mailing," AP NEWS (Associated Press, July 15, 2021), https://apnews.com/article/lifestyle-entertainment-business-arts-and-entertainment-amazoncom-inc-26035c9ee8c2720d1bd2dc7983b0 35f3.

223. Abigail Shrier, "Gender Activists Are Trying to Cancel My Book. Why Is Silicon Valley Helping Them?" Quillette (Quillette, November 19, 2020), https://quillette.com/2020/11/07/gender-activists-are-trying-to-cancel-my-book-why-is-silicon-valley-helping-them/.

224. Owen Bowcott, "Judge Rules against Researcher Who Lost Job over Transgender Tweets," The Guardian (Guardian News and Media, December 18, 2019), https://www.theguardian.com/society/2019/dec/18/judge-rules-against-charity-worker-who-lost-job-over-transgender-tweets.

225. Critical Thinkers call it gender "affirmation" surgery.

226. Bhavesh Purohit, "When Transgender Fighter Fallon Fox Broke Her Opponent's Skull in MMA Fight," Sports news (Sportskeeda, September 30, 2021), https://www.sportskeeda.com/mma/news-when-transgender-fighter-fallon-fox-broke-opponent-s-skull-mma-fight.

227. Charmaine Patterson, "Swimmer Lia Thomas, Who Is Transgender, Continues to Break Women's Records," PEOPLE.com, accessed January 6, 2022, https://people.com/sports/upenn-swimmer-lia-thomas-who-is-transgender-continues-to-break-womens-records/.

228. "H.R.5 - 117th Congress (2021-2022): Equality Act," Congress.gov, accessed November 18, 2021, https://www.congress.gov/bill/117th-congress/house-bill/5.

229. "Just in: Abigail Shrier, Author of Book on Gender Dysphoria, Slams Equality Act," YouTube (Forbes Breaking News, March 17, 2021), https://www.youtube.com/watch?v=fquL1y0QAM4.

230. "Equality Act Now," HRC (Human Rights Campaign), accessed November 18, 2021, https://www.hrc.org/campaigns/equality-act.

231. Brittany Bernstein, "Lawsuit Accuses California of Endangering Female Prisoners by Forcing Them to Share Housing with Biological Males,"

Yahoo! Sports (Yahoo!), accessed November 18, 2021, https://sports.yahoo.com/lawsuit-accuses-california-endangering-female-223614041.html.

232. ibid

233. "Just in: Abigail Shrier, Author of Book on Gender Dysphoria, Slams Equality Act," YouTube (Forbes Breaking News, March 17, 2021), https://www.youtube.com/watch?v=fquL1y0QAM4.

234. Frank Bruni, "These Campus Inquisitions Must Stop," The New York Times (The New York Times, June 3, 2017), https://www.nytimes.com/2017/06/03/opinion/sunday/bruni-campus-inquisitions-evergreen-state.html.

235. Dorian S. Abbot and Ivan Marinovic, "The Diversity Problem on Campus: Opinion," Newsweek (Newsweek, August 12, 2021), https://www.newsweek.com/diversity-problem-campus-opinion-1618419.

236. Harald Schmidt, Lawrence O. Gostin, and Michelle A. Williams, "Is It Lawful and Ethical to Prioritize Racial Minorities for Covid-19 Vaccines?," JAMA (JAMA Network, November 24, 2020), https://jamanetwork.com/journals/jama/fullarticle/2771874.

237. Phil Galewitz, "Vermont to Give Minority Residents Vaccine Priority," Kaiser Health News, April 5, 2021, https://khn.org/news/article/vermont-gives-blacks-and-other-minority-residents-vaccine-priority/.

238. Samantha Artiga, Nambi Ndugga, and Olivia Pham, "How Are States Addressing Racial Equity in Covid-19 Vaccine Efforts?" KFF, March 10, 2021, https://www.kff.org/racial-equity-and-health-policy/issue-brief/how-are-states-addressing-racial-equity-in-covid-19-vaccine-efforts/.

239. Rong-Gong Lin II and Luke Money, "California Will Reserve 40% of COVID-19 Vaccine for Disadvantaged Areas to Speed Reopenings," Los Angeles Times (Los Angeles Times, March 4, 2021), https://www.latimes.com/california/story/2021-03-03/california-will-reserve-40-of-covid-19-vaccine-for-needy-in-push-to-speed-reopenings.

240. "Racism, Health Injustice and Health Care Workforce Training," Mayo Clinic, July 16, 2020, https://www.mayo.edu/research/centers-programs/center-for-health-equity-community-engagement-research/racism-health-injustice-health-care-workforce-training.

241. Ibram X. Kendi, "IDEA: Pass an Antiracist Constitutional Amendment," POLITICO, accessed December 8, 2021, https://www.politico.com/interactives/2019/how-to-fix-politics-in-america/inequality/pass-an-antiracist-constitutional-amendment/.

242. Mark Murphy, "'The More Justice, the Less Freedom': Max Horkheimer on Critical Theory," Social Theory Applied, accessed December 14, 2021, https://socialtheoryapplied.com/2014/10/03/4204/.

243. James Copland, "Critical Race Theory Briefing Book," Christopher F. Rufo, accessed December 17, 2021, https://christopherrufo.com/crt-briefing-book/.

244. Nsba, "NSBA Letter to Federal Gov't," MDJOnline.com, October 6, 2021, https://www.mdjonline.com/nsba-letter-to-federal-govt/pdf_4b147a5a-26b2-11ec-8e78-8b9b2977ef49.html.

Printed in Great Britain
by Amazon

39452538R00116